Can You Go?

Can You Go?

*Assessments and Program Design for the
Active Athlete and Everybody Else*

Dan John

Foreword
Chad Harbach

On Target Publications
Santa Cruz, California

Can You Go?
Assessments and Program Design for the Active Athlete and Everybody Else

Dan John

Foreword by Chad Harbach

ISBN-13: 978-1-931046-74-9
First printing May 2015

On Target Publications
P O Box 1335
Aptos, California 95001 USA
www.otpbooks.com

Library of Congress Cataloging-in-Publication Data

John, Dan, 1957–
Can you go? : assessments and program design for the active athlete and
  everybody else / Dan John ; foreword by Chad Harbach.
    pages cm
Includes index.
ISBN 978-1-931046-74-9
1. Athletes—Training of. 2. Coaching (Athletics)—Study and teaching.
  3. Personal trainers—Study and teaching. I. Title.
GV711.5.J65 2015
796.07'7—dc23
                        2015007672

Also by Dan John

Intervention

Never Let Go

Mass Made Simple

From Dad to Grad

Easy Strength (with Pavel Tsatsouline)

Fat Loss Happens on Monday (with Josh Hillis)

Dedication

To Kelly and Lindsay—
For everything, every day

To my brother, Gary—
For always being there

To my friends who died that August day—
Long Live the Brotherhood

Contents

Foreword

I FIRST STUMBLED ACROSS Dan John's work in 2012, a year I spent traveling on a book tour and living out of hotels. The hotels didn't have gyms, and when they did I was too beat to use them. My workouts involved a few pushups before breakfast and plenty of pint curls after dinner, plus many hours crunched into a middle airplane seat.

At least I was doing a lot of suitcase walks, though I didn't have a name for them yet.

No doubt because I felt deprived of physical exertion, I found myself, in rare down moments, lying half-asleep on the hotel bed, reading about physical exertion. Through who-knows-what labyrinth of link-clicking, I found an article by a guy named Dan John. Its clarity—its simplicity—stopped me short: Here, plain as your nose, was the truth about working out.

Soon I hopped up to test whatever the article suggested— Bulgarian goat bag swings, I think. Reading Dan's work has a way of getting you up on your feet, or down on the floor.

I clicked to a second article, and a third. I went to his blog and immersed myself. I had yet to handle a kettlebell or fix my appalling squat form, but already I knew I'd found what I'd been seeking. Every hard-won insight I'd brushed up against, in three decades of thinking about sports and fitness, was present in every line he wrote.

When my travels ended, I began to practice what Dan preached. Of course, I got stronger and fitter. But more than that, I started thinking about how my fitness fit with everything else. If my weight training and my martial arts practice seemed sometimes to work against each other, instead of harmonizing...well, why was that? Were my workouts making me more energetic? More resilient? Was my mind getting stronger? Was my writing improving?

Under Dan's tutelage, I fixed my squat. I stretched my hamstrings and learned to hinge. I bought a kettlebell. I bought a bigger kettlebell. I worked out easier and easier, and harder and harder. I read like-minded experts and attended seminars. I got—am getting—better and stronger. Not younger—I hope he includes that trick in his next book—but better and stronger.

As much as I value Dan's programs and protocols and practical insights, what strikes me most about his work is the method and quality of the thinking.

Dan is fond of saying that "the body is one piece." You could say the same thing about his body of work. The blog, the articles, the interviews, the books—it's all one piece.

That work has a bracing clarity that's instantly recognizable. It's the clarity that comes from thinkers who spend their entire lives in direct, empirical engagement with a subject they love. These people bring to their work as much humility and as few preconceived ideas as possible. Ideas emerge from observation, and not vice versa.

What works—both for themselves and, usually, for many others—comes to the fore. Everything else drops away. What remains is a humane, flexible, systematic, nondogmatic approach. The job becomes, as Einstein had it, "as simple as possible, but no simpler."

Whenever I find such thinkers, I cling to their work, not just for what I can learn about the subject at hand—the subject is almost irrelevant—but for what I can learn about how to live, how to think, how to approach situations.

There are examples, of course, in every field. I'm not a kindergarten teacher or a six-year-old, but I can happily reread Maria Montessori's books on education, because her writing is grounded in years of patient observation of the dirt-poor Italian kids she was tasked with teaching—a startling number of those kids learned to read at age four.

I've never written a screenplay, but *Story* by Robert McKee, who's honed his screenwriting seminar over decades, grasps the form so deeply that I constantly refer to its insights. In fiction, it's hard to beat Chekhov for the clarity of his insight into human behavior.

And in strength and fitness, it's hard to beat Dan John. I wish like heck somebody had told me about his work in 1981, when I started playing organized sports (I was five), or at least in 1996, when I started lifting weights, but oh well. At least I know it now.

Chad Harbach
NY Times Best Selling Author of *The Art of Fielding*

Chapter **1**

Assessing the Question, What Do You Want?

Introduction

Part of my job is to ask people, "What do you want?"

I'm not a department-store Santa; I'm a strength coach. Some might think I have a magic bag filled with goodies designed to strip bodyfat and build lean body mass, but instead I have just a handful of tools.

Knowing what we want is essential in setting our goals. We need to know where we are when heading on this journey. The answers to *What do you want?* are usually tame—

♦ "I want to get leaner and have abs like I see on TV."

- ◆ "I want to look better and feel better. I want to have more energy."
- ◆ "I want to look like I did at age (fill in the blank)."
- ◆ "I want a pony."

That last one is how my wife Tiffini always answers the question. Honestly, it might be the easiest of the four outcomes to achieve.

Here's the truth: The answer isn't what we want; it's what we *need*.

Often, I know what we need to do. The issue is usually simple. Rarely do my clients and athletes know what's needed. My first hurdle is to overcome this gap.

If I could summarize excellent coaching or teaching into one phrase, it would be this—

It's not what the coach knows;
it's what the athlete knows.

You could replace coach and athlete for dance teacher and dancer, trainer and client or conductor and musician.

I'm striving to teach my athletes and clients that when I say, "This is what we need to focus on now," we can agree to what "this" actually is. And that "this" is what that person needs.

It might not be what the person wants.

What follows in this book is my attempt to address a better way to help people with their fitness, health and longevity goals. Rather than focus on what each client *wants*, let's turn this toward what the client *needs*.

It might be possible to define happiness as that place where our wants and needs are both the same. Many people have no idea what they need. At the same time, their list of wants may cover several volumes.

I want that pony, but I need to do my mobility work and eat my vegetables.

In the past few years, I've come up with a simple method of assessing clients to get right to this core question: *What do we need to do?*

The *1-2-3-4 Assessment* that follows in this book will efficiently and quickly answer that question.

The assessment also answers the next difficult question facing coaches and trainers: *What do we do next?*

That's a question we'll address with the *Five Tools of Fitness and Nutrition.*

The assessment is simple and repeatable. It can be done with one person or hundreds. It answers the most important question in fitness—

What do we need to do?

If a person is trying to get back in shape, the answer might be obvious. Perhaps it's to get a few workouts that combine mobility and strength and to increase vegetable intake.

Now, for an athlete with an upcoming event, we have to look the person sternly in the eye and ask another question, "Can you go?"

Those three words, *Can you go?,* are the great challenge of sport and life. When your child needs you, you rally up and take care of business even if you have the flu or have not a minute to spare.

For the athlete, this is the time to step up, step in, grab the ball and go.

Can you go?

To answer this question under the heat of competition takes years of training, growth and preparation. The lessons we've learned from athletes help us lead the typical clients toward their goals, too.

Chapter 2

Constant Assessment

Interconnected Truths

The first step toward helping our clients achieve their goals in fitness is to help them figure out who they are right here and right now.

In fitness, success comes down to two interconnected truths—

- Everything works. Every diet, fad, program and gimmick works.

- Everything works for about six weeks. Every gimmick usually has the tagline of two weeks, or worse, overnight, and then…it stops working. Most people have learned this lesson many times.

These two truths lead us to the question that comes up on week seven, day one, *"What do I do next?"*

In setting a goal, using a simple assessment and a sense of where we are today (not twenty years ago!), we can answer the question, "What do I do next?"

It is simple. But, it's not easy.

John Powell, a former world-record holder in the discus, has an insightful story about this point. Powell had been teaching a group of young men how to throw the discus. He was emphasizing how simple the movement is across the ring: *1-2-3*.

One boy attempted it, crossed his feet and fell to the ground.

"You said it was easy," he complained.

John countered, "I said it was simple, not easy."

The answer is simple. It may or may not be easy.

Let's find out where your client is first. Then, we address what to do next.

Assessments: Judging Progression and Programs without Hyperbole

There's an important question to ask yourself about everything in life: *Did it work?*

Away from the glitch and sparkle of advertising, BS sessions and bravado with friends, did "it" work?

Here's how I usually know it worked: I did it.

Fill in anything you want for *it:* life hacks, gasoline-saving tricks, window-cleaning tips, odd food combinations or exotic training programs. I think peanut butter on a hamburger is excellent. If it works, it works.

Getting an idea, implementing the idea and looking at the results define life, learning and lifting. In one word—assessments—we can sum up where a client is and how the results are coming along.

Goals and assessments live in this yin and yang whirl: It's great to have goals, but where are we now? Did anything we did in the past week, month or year bring us closer to the goal?

I believe in assessments. I often joke that we should be like the character from the Harry Potter series, Mad-Eye Moody. He would yell at the kids, "Constant vigilance!"

Replace "vigilance" with "assessment," and you will be a better coach, teacher and trainer. Constant assessment!

If there's a must to coaching, it's this: You *must* assess. Vladimir Janda said this half a century ago, "Time spent in assessments will save time in treatment," or in our case, in training.

It's true: If there's a key to coaching, it's understanding that "here" is a moving target. I hope we established "there" already, the "B" of A–B. "A," of course, is where the goal setter is now. And, let me restate the cliché: If you don't know where you're going, any road will get you there.

We want to be on the road to mastery, even if we don't make every goal we set. In this, I often quote Cervantes: "The road is always better than the inn."

We should write A–B as A TO B with capital letters screaming out the path. Simply getting on the path to appropriate, legal and worthy goals leads me to places I never imagined. If the road is leading you to a worthy destination (thank you, Earl Nightingale), there are many wonderful stops along the way.

In short, strive for mastery—or, better yet, strive for the road *to* mastery.

When someone has a goal that is A–B, things are pretty easy. Attaining a goal is a lot like sailing a boat into the wind. You'll tack back and forth with the goal to your right, then to your left, then back to your right. But these are course corrections; you're always advancing forward toward the goal.

Your job as the coach is to shout out, "Bring it around!" every so often to get your clients back on target.

For those still struggling with an appropriate goal—these would be our A–Z friends—assessments show the progress. The A–Z people often have goals that are so difficult and demand so much time, energy and investment that the little steps are going to feel like failure.

The mother of three who wants to look like the cover of a fitness magazine in six weeks is thinking Z, not B. Sometimes, our task is to point to logical, reasonable, attainable goals. This doesn't mean Z is impossible, but let's start with some movement in the right direction first.

There's another kind of goal we call "A/Not A."

Steve Ledbetter came up with this insight: Many people don't know what they want in fitness, body composition or health, but they do know they don't want to be "here." These people say, "This is how I look today, but this isn't who I am!"

Assessment allows us to reaffirm that they're not where they started. Once they were "here," but now they can point backward and argue that they aren't at that "here" anymore—indeed, that old "here" is getting farther away.

Assessment should clue us into one important point. The impact of training should be obvious. *The impact of training should push toward the goal, and it should help achieve the goal.*

And most people know this.

Sadly, most people's training seems to not do anything at all to support the goals.

Instead, people tend to do what my mom used to call "monkey see, monkey do." It's a rare week when I'm not asked a question about something training-related that was seen on the internet or on television that looks fun and interesting. That's all fine, but it rarely supports the goals of the person asking the question.

The Basics of the Quadrants

I can't repeat the idea of the Quadrants often enough. These Quadrants are my attempt to answer the question: "What is the impact of a strength coach?"

My original answer, "It depends," wasn't very enlightening. In my book *Intervention*, I explained how the idea of Quadrants clarified my understanding of how a coach or trainer can lead people to their goals. If you haven't read it already (and I thank you if you have!), see that book for a longer study of this concept.

A client's location in the Qs depends first on the number of qualities the goal requires—for example, playing football requires many qualities, but shot putting requires only two: get strong and throw the shot.

Second, the Qs relate to the absolute highest levels at which humanity can perform.

I wish you luck trying to figure out how to train for elite sprinting and elite swimming at the same time.

Quadrant I	Quadrant III
Physical education class—*lots of low-level qualities*	Most people—*few qualities, at a low level*
Quadrant II	Quadrant IV
Collision sports, certain occupations—*lots of high-level qualities*	Rare athletic competition—*few qualities, at the highest level*

Quadrant I represents that wonderful period of youth when we learn movement, games and sports. I hope you learned to swim and ride a bike, as these are harder to learn as you age. Once we leave the primary and secondary years of school, we leave QI behind.

Quadrant II gets all the press. Collision sports and collision occupations tend to bring out our desire to be superheroes. It takes a special kind of person, in both mental toughness and physical gifts, to be the best of the best, and few have long careers doing these kinds of jobs. Professional football players and Navy SEALs are amazing. Businesses use the image of them to sell a lot of books and magazines to people who want to be like them.

I'm going to just say this right now: *You aren't in QII.*

Usually, if you were at one time, you're not anymore, nor are most of the clients we'll ever train.

Most people are in Quadrant III. There are only a few physical qualities needed to train in this quadrant, and the levels are comparably low.

Fat loss can be defined as caloric restriction and inefficient movement. There are only two qualities here, and picking the appropriate approach to these qualities can ensure success. This approach might not always be what someone wants to do. A bad dancer burns more calories in a dance class than a good dancer, and a crappy bike takes more effort to move than a good bike. Inefficient movement might not be as fun as mastering a sport, but it does ensure successful fat loss.

Usually when I walk people through the assessment, I tell them they're in Quadrant III. It's not laziness; it's reality. Sure, an NFL player *was* in Quadrant II, but as a career moves on, training simplifies.

There's a sad but true moment for everyone as I walk through an assessment: You're not in high school or college anymore!

Quadrant IV demands the hand of God, as I like to joke. A person has to be born a sprinter or an elite lifter *and* be blessed to be in a location that supports sprinting or lifting. A boy born with the genetic gifts to be the greatest lifter of all time who was raised in Iowa might end up being an outstanding wrestler. Put that same kid in certain towns in North Dakota, and we have a solid hockey player. Now, if he was born in Bulgaria or China, he becomes a multiple world-champion lifter.

The problem I always had in the past in explaining QIII, where most people belong, was that I lumped Olympic athletes into the same group as the person trying to lose five pounds. They're both QIII, but there's enough distinction between the two to break them into smaller groups: active (or aging) athletes and everybody else.

For shorthand, I refer to active athletes as A^2 and everybody else as E^2.

Active (Aging) Athletes

Training plans for the QIII A^2, our active athletes, are simple: The athlete needs to practice the sport and then do fundamental human movements in the weightroom with the appropriate reps, sets and loads.

The focus in strength training will be to address weaknesses, but as athletes, we want to compete with our strengths.

Yes, it *is* that simple.

Some active athletes will do complex movements such as the Olympic lifts. Others will find that the basic movements—planks and goblet squats, for example—will support their goals. If there are lagging movement or joint mobility issues, some specialized training might be valuable for periods of the year.

Gaps in training or lack of attaining the basic standards in the fundamentals will become more glaring as the athlete ages.

Additionally, these issues will also diminish the chances of achieving the highest goals because elite performance demands so much from the body.

In truth, the QIII A^2 needs to master the techniques, tactics and strategies necessary to perform at the highest possible level. The strength coach supports this by providing a balanced, strong platform to launch the athlete toward the goal.

Training the QIII athlete is a balancing act. Since lifting weights has become a part of every athlete's training, athletes are much bigger and stronger than ever before. Athletes seem to get bigger every year. In the 1960s, offensive linemen in the NFL were still in the 210–230-pound range, and rarely did you see a 300-pounder. Today, many high schools have 300-pounders.

For the QIII A^2, one of the hardest things to teach about strength is when enough is enough. Tom Fahey once studied the strength levels of an elite discus thrower. According to him, an elite thrower needs to be able to do these lifts—

- 400-pound bench press

- 450-pound back squat

- 250-pound snatch

- 300-pound clean

To the average person, these are big lifts, but to elite throwers, these are almost light—and to some, these are poor lifts!

Getting stronger, along with getting more flexible, is one of the easiest things to achieve. Lift weights and we will get stronger. The issue for the QIII athletes is this: As they continue to increase strength, they *must* see a corresponding improvement in sport performance.

Lifting is the easy part of the formula for improved performance. To improve or maintain elite levels of performance, the athlete must remain fresh enough to train.

And, yes, I know you know that. But applying this truth is hard.

Strength coaches who work with QIII athletes must focus on two things—

- ♦ **Are there any gaps in the training program?** Are the athletes doing all the fundamental human movements? Is there a balance in load and volume in these movements?

- ♦ **Is the athlete up to the standards in these movements?** The levels for track and field are known through a large body of experience and research. And other sports are quickly catching up in this area.

Every other quality an athlete needs should come from practicing and performing the sport. As I always say about being a good head track-and-field coach, "Throwers throw. Jumpers jump. Hurdlers hurdle."

If a soccer player hasn't kicked a ball in months but can deadlift three times bodyweight, someone's missing the point.

With the QIII A^2, we must have a laser-beam focus on the goal. The most important key is to cut back the options. Insist on less variety in the weightroom, focus on quality reps, and apply appropriate load. Enough is enough. I remind my athletes, "You're making progress here, so *let's stick to the process.*"

One of the most common errors in training is to start questioning the process. This often happens after an athlete reads or hears something new and exciting, but we must trust the process…trust the path. Let the process happen, and—something that doesn't happen as often as I wish—*finish the process.*

Even if you or your clients aren't athletes, there's a lot of value in listening to the sports world. There are some things in elite performance that we've learned the hard way, and you might as well enjoy the free knowledge.

For example, as an athlete, traveling is always an issue. Many athletes are built funny: too big, too long and too wide for normal airplane seats, to name one problem. The traveling athlete has the same issue as a typical office worker—with prolonged sitting, the body begins to round forward, the hips tighten and we seem to get glued to some type of monitor screen.

There are three things I recommend for traveling athletes the moment they get into their hotel rooms—

1. Stretch the hip flexors.
2. Work on thoracic spine mobility.
3. Try a few bird dogs, and test the single-side bird dog to reestablish rotary stability.

Universally, traveling athletes suffer from tight hip flexors, stiff t-spines and a loss of rotary stability. Before they step up to the plate with a guy throwing something at them at ninety-five miles per hour—or doing whatever it is they do—I recommend getting back toward "more normal."

As one of my baseball players noted, he was shocked to see how stable he was with bird dogs when at home, and how completely that vanished during plane rides.

Even if these little stretching and mobility movements are just voodoo, I'm fine with that, too. If I just make a dancer believe we took the mileage out of her body and now she's good to go, that's pretty good. I'm convinced everyone needs to do these few correctives every day, unless you walk and move all day with no lengthy periods of sitting.

Learn from the elites, stretch a bit and test those bird dogs daily.

Athletes can also teach the rest of us that superior performance comes from not trying so hard. In World War II, fighter pilots were having a problem not recognizing friend or foe quickly enough. Among others, Bud Winters was hired to help them deal with this issue. Using his sports background, he discovered that physical relaxation leads to mental relaxation, which in turn brought quicker recognition in the sky.

Years later, he became the head track-and-field coach of the legendary San Jose State teams known as Speed City. His program was better than nearly every national team in the world, and his athletes led the world in sprints, discus throws and pole vaults. He called this method of relaxation *Relax and Win*.

He expected his athletes to learn to fall asleep, on demand, anytime and anywhere. He used physical warmups to produce more relaxation. He believed that a loose, relaxed effort was superior to trying to kill yourself for victory. It works—and not only in sports. We also find these benefits in business, public speaking and normal human interactions.

At the same time, Eastern European sports scientists were discovering that everyone can tense at about the same rate, but that superior athletes can relax their muscles faster. They theorized that relaxation was the secret to elite performance.

So relax. We're doing fine.

The next great lesson we can all learn from elite performance is simple: Getting stronger by lifting weights can improve every aspect of life. Yes, our athletes will throw farther and jump higher, and that's great, thank you very much. But they'll also move the couch easier, carry in more groceries faster, and generally be more of a help than a hindrance in daily life.

That, by the way, is nicer for the rest of us, too.

Can You Go?

I have a sad truth about QIII athletes and assessments. It all comes down to one question: *Can you go?*

It's a phrase we use in American football, a fundamental question that means "can you play or not?" If you walk up to me on the day of Nationals and tell me about the lousy dinner, crappy hotel and rough commute, I'll smile and nod and act like I listened to all of that, and then I'll ask you, "Can you go?"

If you can, then get in your uniform, begin your warmups and let's get going.

If you can't, it's over—let's go home. We're finished here today. I hope you learned something from all the preparation, but we're through now. I'm sorry. You can go home. It's over.

I wish I could be kinder, but athletics can be cruel. As athletes, we have to be sure to ask ourselves this question often—*Can you go?*—and not wait for the morning of something important to wonder why we started the effort in the first place.

This leads us to a small but important question: Is everyone an athlete?

George Sheehan, the famous writer and runner, once noted: "Being fit is one thing. Being an athlete is another. Fitness is the ability to do work. Being an athlete is something quite different. Fitness is what you pass through on the way to a superior physical, mental and spiritual state."

As much as I love his work, I've always felt this line made athletes and athletics too important. While fitness, I agree, is the ability to do work or to do a task, Phil Maffetone, whom I count on for much of my understanding about cardiovascular conditioning, wrote a book called *Everyone Is an Athlete*, which argues an opposing standpoint.

I, however, will take the middle ground for once, because I think both have valid points.

We have to meet people where they are in life. If I ask you the question, "Can you go?," and you answer, "Where?," I need another set of assessment tools.

Everybody Else

It's time to look at E^2—everybody else.

There's a joke that's been hanging around education for a few decades. A fish, a bird and a monkey are all standing in line. A guy with a clipboard says, "Okay, it's time for the basic assessment. Let's see who can climb a tree the fastest."

The fish says it can't get out of its bowl or it will die.

"You fail then."

The bird asks to fly to the top, and the guy responds, "No, the test says climb, not fly. You must follow the protocol."

The monkey wins by climbing the fastest, and gets the job—to climb a tower and look out for enemy ships approaching the land. Of course, this is a job that a flyer or a swimmer might have been better doing.

Somehow, I think this story is a fair warning about assessments and readiness.

The assessments for QIII E^2 are based on experience and on the study of both elite athletes and of polio victims.

Polio was a feared disease throughout much of the early- to middle-twentieth century, and the work of two of the researchers combating the disease remains relevant today. The concept of progressive resistance exercise, developed by Tom DeLorme, remains the key to understanding strength training. And Vladimir Janda's contributions and insights about certain muscles shrinking with age or disease, and other muscles weakening with age and disease, continue to be the best approach to total-body training.

Elite athletes note that while traveling they lose hip-flexor flexibility, as well as have issues with t-spine mobility and rotary stability. Janda showed us decades ago that the tonics—the muscles that tighten with age or illness—need to be stretched. These are the pectorals, the biceps, the hip flexors and the hamstrings, among others. After sitting in a chair, these are the muscles you want to stretch back into place when you stand up.

Paul Anderson, a fine weightlifter from the 1950s and '60s, once noted: "The guy with the biggest butt lifts the biggest weights." Janda found that the glutes, along with the deltoids, triceps and abdominal wall, were a person's seat of power. These are the muscles you would use if you had to run down some game with a stick or a rock in preparation for dinner.

As we age, these muscles weaken and need strengthening, and this is another time when the strength coach becomes important.

Finally, the great tradition in lifting from the pre–anabolic-steroid age recognized the importance of keeping the rep range around fifteen to twenty-five for most movements. Reg Park, one of history's great bodybuilders, recommended five sets of five for strength and power. The DeLorme protocols call for about the same number of total reps per movement during a training session. The important thing about these three points is clear: From the elite training halls to the rehab wing, we learn the same basic keys to success in training.

+ Stretch what is tightening.

+ Strengthen what is weakening.

+ Do both with the least amount of work.

Keeping the Goal in Mind

As we begin to consider the assessment, we'll measure the standard things like height, weight and waist measurement, but I'd like to ask you to actually *use* these measurements. I call this approach the *1-2-3-4 Assessment*—we're going to dive into that in the next chapter.

Mentally, I want you to have two thoughts as you begin an assessment—

+ No ice cream

+ Be a forthteller, not a fortune teller

What in the world does that mean?

A few years ago, Payton Manning would step up to the line of scrimmage and yell out "Ice cream!" Now, this wasn't as famous as "Omaha, Omaha," but I discovered from one of my trainees who won a Super Bowl ring with the Colts that ice cream had a special meaning: "Everything I'm about to say, ignore." Manning would then point at the other team and yell lots of words, numbers and colors, and none of it meant anything.

When someone hands me a business card that reads "The World's Finest Coach," or "The World's Finest Personal Trainer," what I actually see is "ice cream."

Make sure your assessment isn't just a bunch of ice cream. Don't use it as a way to entice clients or to send out the illusion of professionalism. Assessments can literally save lives. Assessments are the first line of defense against injuries in the gym.

Assessments are important.

Occasionally, we assess what we do in the gym. We ask our people, "Do we do what we say we do, or are we just barking 'ice cream'?"

The next thought to hold in your head is that you're a forth-teller—this is X; this is Y. You are *not* a fortuneteller! When asked, "What does X mean?" you need to answer "X."

That's our job. Our job is not to guess that someone's bones are all pointing to a future filled with back squats. Assess! Don't guess. Don't try to predict the future.

Besides, as Niels Bohr said, "Prediction is very difficult, especially about the future."

Illuminate. Project. Point. That's the role of the assessment tests.

Chapter 3

The 1-2-3-4 Assessment

The Big Circles

For all QIII clients—athletes or everyone else—I use a Venn diagram to help address which of the three most important qualities need to be stressed in training and lifestyle: joint mobility, body composition and strength gaps.

Joint mobility concerns the ability of each joint to move freely. Enough is enough with joint mobility; if a joint is moving pain-free through a full range of motion, it's enough. There's no need for circus tricks.

Body composition is the search for lean body mass—more muscle and less fat.

And addressing strength gaps through strength training improves the quality of life for the elderly, the injured and the ill—and it can do wonders for everybody else, too.

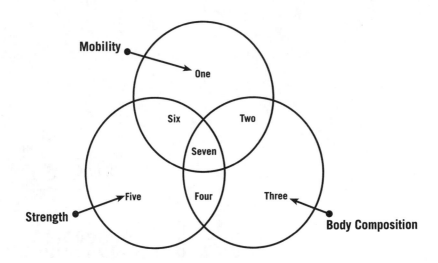

In my Venn diagram for the assessments, there are three big circles, and each represents one of the most important qualities in training—mobility, body comp and strength. Pure mobility is a *One*; body comp is a *Three*; and strength is a *Five*. Some clients will need to focus on just one of these, some clients on two and some on all three.

When I work with aging collision athletes and collision occupation groups, for example, I focus on *Six*. I consider a QII athlete "old" after about age twenty-six, by the way, because the years of training, competing and working tend to do a fair amount of aging to the system. People can only take so many hits before they don't recover as well. In *Six*, we train strength and joint mobility back-to-back throughout the training session—that is, every strength movement has a joint mobility movement connected to it.

As we progress, you'll notice that clients who fall into *Seven* are actually quite easy to work with in both training and lifestyle. Addressing one issue—for example, joint mobility—may help these clients sleep better and longer, which is often helpful for body comp. A little less fat and a more muscle helps strength training, which in turn builds a better platform for joint mobility. In the early weeks, *Sevens* often make the best progress of all, as the basic principle of "everything works" holds true for them in this stage.

The Seven QIII E² Subgroups

Each of the seven subgroups requires a different focus on specific issues, along with an equal focus on making fitness and health habits. These focuses are as follows—

+ *Ones:* Hypertrophy and mobility training

+ *Twos:* Hypertrophy and mobility training; nutrition and caloric restriction; inefficient exercise

+ *Threes:* Nutrition and caloric restriction; inefficient exercise

+ *Fours:* Strength training; nutrition and caloric restriction; inefficient exercise

+ *Fives:* Strength training

+ *Sixes:* Strength training; hypertrophy and mobility training

+ *Sevens:* Hypertrophy and mobility training; strength training; nutrition and caloric restriction; inefficient exercise

The Assessments

Assessment One: Stand on One Foot

The first test of our assessment is so fundamental, you may miss its importance.

Ask your client to stand on one foot. If the person can stand on one foot for over ten seconds, great; move along to the next assessment. Ideally, we're looking for a range between ten and twenty seconds. Anything beyond twenty seconds is not really important. Give a hearty handshake and say, "Good for you."

If the next person stands for less than ten seconds, it's time to outsource—refer the client to a medical doctor.

Years ago, Clarence Bass quoted this on his excellent website, *cbass.com*: "As with muscles, the balance system needs to be challenged in order to improve." That came from Scott McCredie's book, *Balance: In Search of the Lost Sense.*

After reading the quote, I thought back over my time as a coach and trainer, and I began to link up little stories about clients who struggled with balance. One had MS and often had a small stumble when moving around the gym. Another was well over three hundred pounds and couldn't find his balancing point.

In 1991, one of my clients, a successful real estate magnate, asked me about a painful ankle.

"Did you step off a curb wrong or something?"

"No."

"Do you remember hurting it?"

"No."

"Do me a favor and go see a doctor, would you?"

He did. He had prostate cancer, and they discovered it early enough that he still comes by every so often to train with me. Why did his ankle hurt? I don't know. I don't care. By getting to see the doctor early, he took care of the big problem.

Why can't someone stand on one foot for ten seconds? I don't know. I don't care. Go see the doctor.

By the way, everyone I know starts practicing standing on one foot after being tested. That's a win–win for a coach: The client is seeking mastery outside the confines of the gym. It makes for a fun test and is something worth doing when you're just standing in line for a movie or doing a kitchen chore. Does it have the value of the other tests? Well, who knows, but it takes only about a minute (at most!), and it might be challenging enough to get someone excited about improving other areas of training.

Test both feet to get a sense of things. Often, one side might stagger a bit more than the other, and that's worthy of further discussion, too.

But as we begin, let's just stick to the ten-second standard.

If the person fails, ask him or her to return after the visit with the doctor. Then, continue on to the second assessment.

Assessment Two: Measurements

The "2" in the *1-2-3-4 Assessment* refers to assessing two measurements. The first is weight. Have your client hop on the scale. If the scale tilts *under* three hundred pounds, continue assessing. If the measure is *over* three hundred pounds, refer out.

According to my doctor, Ross Brunetti, once someone gets over three hundred pounds, the rules change. If you're twenty-five years old and you don't smoke and you wear your seat belt, you will very likely live to at least fifty-five years of age (statistics are statistics), but if you weigh over three hundred pounds, in the words of Lee Corso, "not so fast." Mortality rates for people over three hundred pounds are different.

When a client is over three hundred pounds, refer to three professionals: an eye doctor, a dentist and a medical doctor.

Aside from the obvious benefits of a yearly eye exam—I strongly recommend this for everyone—there are some other benefits, too. An eye doctor can see diabetes via damage to the blood vessels, can see evidence of high blood pressure and can get a general sense of the cardiovascular system.

My dentist, Seth Spangler, added the next piece to the obesity puzzle with a simple insight. He told me, after reading one of my articles, "I don't see a lot of obese patients."

I followed up on this and discovered that the problem is most likely twofold. First, there's a serious lack of discussion and teaching in dentistry about dealing with the obese population. This is being addressed, and much of the discussion is based on larger chairs and other accommodations.

The second issue is interesting as it involves a "chicken or the egg" question: If you have bad teeth, will you eat softer, more easily chewed food? Does poor dental health make it more difficult to eat those wonderful colorful vegetables we're always suggesting, while the client instead turns to rolls with margarine? Cardboard carbs—the chips and boxed-food family—turn into mush in the mouth, no chewing necessary.

Could better tooth care be part of the issue with obesity? It's worth discussion. It's worth a semi-annual visit to the dentist.

Finally, and there's no surprise here, I'd like this client to see a medical doctor. If this is the third appointment after the eye doctor and dentist, there might not be a lot of surprises left. Blood tests, blood pressure and other simple tests might highlight some long-term issues.

I'm not qualified in any way to do medical exams, so I send the client off to get all of these checked. Does it bring me peace of mind or a surety that we won't have issues? Not really. I'm not worried about sudden death in the gym. What I want to do is ensure that the client gets a sense of a whole-body approach to dealing with fitness, health and longevity. If there are serious issues found, or even simple things like cavities in the teeth, we're well on our way to addressing problems.

If the person can stand on one foot and weighs under three hundred pounds, we can start truly assessing how to determine the proper approach to the fitness goals.

The Second Measurement

The next step is simple: Measure the height and waistline.

Always measure height. It's an amazing number for assessing performance at the minimum levels; we'll talk more about this later.

"Keeping your waist circumference to less than half your height can help increase life expectancy for every person in the world," according to Margaret Ashwell, an independent consultant and former science director of the British Nutrition Foundation. Brad Pilon, of *Eat Stop Eat* fame, discusses this issue at length in his digital book, *Dieting for Muscle Growth*. He takes this a step further and notes that if your waist is over the one-half measure of your height, you might be suffering from a variety of inflammation issues.

What it boils down to is this: If a person is over that number, whatever you do to reduce this waist measurement is going to be better. Or…get taller!

Again quoting Dr. Ashwell, "Abdominal fat affects organs like the heart, liver and kidneys more adversely than fat around the hips and bottom, in terms of cardiometabolic risk."

That's good enough for me—and the test is so simple and fast to set up and explain, it's worthy of instant adoption. If a client's waist-to-height ratio is greater than 1 to 2, the person is a body composition client, regardless of whether the client is male or female.

And, of course, make sure to find the narrowest part of the abdominal area to measure as the waist.

For clarity, let me give you some examples of passing marks—

- ♦ 72 inches tall with a 36-inch waistline

- ♦ 64 inches tall with a 32-inch waistline

- ♦ 68 inches tall with a 33-inch waistline

The following marks would indicate a body composition client, and again, the numbers hold for both men and women—

- ♦ 72 inches tall with a 41-inch waistline

- ♦ 64 inches tall with a 50-inch waistline

- ♦ 68 inches tall with a 50-inch waistline

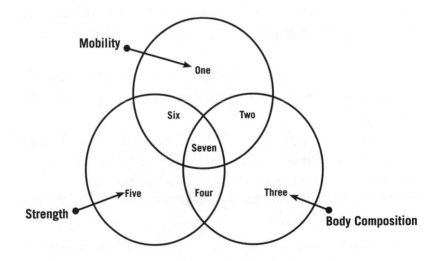

Problems in either of the two measurements indicate a pure body-comp client—this is a *Three* in the Venn Diagram, and we can begin to focus on this immediately.

Assessment Three: Three Questions

Question One: *How many pillows does it take for you to be comfortable at night?*

This single question has led to more pauses in conversations than an off-color joke. If the answer is one, we continue with the assessment. Any more than one, we know the client has joint mobility issues.

The record, by the way, is from a former NFL linebacker who told me he needed nine—yes, nine—pillows to sleep. Imagine trying to sleep next to someone who is constantly trying to get comfortable fussing and fidgeting around nine pillows!

So which joint is the issue? I don't know. But I do know this: As we address movement, we'll probably also be addressing body composition, because joint issues impair a proper sleep cycle.

If you've ever been in pain, you understand this point. A broken limb, a painful back or a pinched nerve in your neck can play havoc on normal sleep. Imagine living years or decades with this pain. Sleep, along with proper dental care, seems to be a missing part of the whole fat-loss formula.

In my other writings, I've discussed some odd sleep experiments I tested to try to lose weight for weightlifting competitions. I once lost thirteen pounds in a week by trying to sleep twelve hours a day. I found it hard to be hungry, and the bodyweight just seemed to fall off. Robb Wolf taught me that all those lights, from LEDs to television screens to street lamps, are interrupting our sleep cycles. Even if you can't sleep twelve hours, darken your bedroom as best you can when you sleep.

As coaches or trainers, we want to monitor how improving movement through the joints and systems help our clients sleep.

Oddly, the easiest way is by counting pillows. Oh, and the client's bedmate will thank us for the changes, too.

In this assessment system, if a client needs more than one pillow, this is a joint mobility client, a *One* on the Venn diagram. It will be rare to find someone who sleeps poorly who doesn't have a body comp issue, too, so many who start with joint mobility will overlap into body comp, making them *Twos*, or likely, *Sevens*.

The upside of working with these people is that addressing either side, joint mobility or body comp, seems to help the other. A little less girth takes a load off the joints and limbs and, in most cases, allows better movement. Better movement tends to lead to more movement, and that's universally a good thing for our goals.

Moreover, some sleep issues improve with body-comp changes, and we begin to see that wonderful cascade where working on something "here" leads to improvement "there."

Question Two: Do you eat colorful vegetables?

The word "colorful" is important. Originally, I left it out, and discovered my mistake. French fries and potato chips might be vegetables, but chomping on red peppers is not the same as chomping on corn chips.

If a client answers, "Yes, why, yes I do," smile and nod. There might be some follow-up questions later—such as how many and how often, and okay, now tell me the truth. Sometimes clients are trying to give you the answer they think you want instead of giving you an honest one.

If a client answers, "Hell, no," at least you know where you stand. Most of us agree that vegetables are a key to health, but this client is going to need to be convinced to join the colorful side.

If a client answers, "Well, what do you mean by vegetable?," you can assume this client isn't eating vegetables.

This question, and the next, aren't used with the Venn diagram, but will give you insights into how to address and work with the client. We'll discuss this in detail later, but let's stay focused on the *1-2-3-4 Assessment* now.

Question Three: *Do you exercise for at least half an hour each day?*

You might find that many people answer yes to this one, but often the other assessments won't match this answer. Don't judge. Some will go down the Socratic Dialogue Avenue—*What do you mean by exercise?*—and this debate will be far more telling than an actual answer.

Honestly, elite athletes will generally answer no. Many elite athletes train often, but with several off days each week. You can actually get into the debate of what is meant by "exercise" in this question, but we're more concerned with the client's response than creating a perfectly clear question.

What we're looking for in the final two questions is the disconnect between the other assessments and the answers to these questions.

If the person claims to eat nothing but healthy meals and snacks, yet is dancing close to obesity numbers, there's more to the story. The first question highlights issues with joint mobility, but the last two give us some insight into the client's mental and emotional processes concerning diet and exercise.

The art of coaching is in understanding and adapting to the client's feelings concerning change. As Coach Maughan told us years ago at Utah State, "Make yourself a slave to good habits."

And, as I've said many times, it's one thing to say that to a room full of Division One athletes, and another to tell that to a single mom juggling everything going on in her life.

We must *hear* our clients and athletes, no matter what they say.

The vegetable and exercise questions allow us some insights that we'll discuss later when assessing what kind of client we have before us—untrained, detrained, daze and confused, overconditioned and untrained, or someone seeking mastery.

Assessment Four: Four Tests

For many clients, at first you'll only need the first test in this group, although certainly, each of the four tests has great value. To determine if clients are on the right path or are going in the wrong direction, it's always helpful to test and see where they are along the way. Tests are also a handy tool to see if the improvements are sticking.

Test One: Plank

The first assessment comes from Stu McGill, the great back expert from Canada. I'm a big fan of all of his work, and I always sit in the front row when he speaks.

The test is very simple: Can the client do a two-minute plank? If not, this is an issue. Either, Stu tells us, the client is training the core poorly or is obese. That's why I love Stu's work; he uses his research facility to bring clarity into my training gym.

Here's a fun tip—I get a very high fail rate when I let clients know they're halfway through the test. That groan and feeling of "No way!" sends people dropping out of the challenge. It often takes a few attempts to mentally prepare a person for a two-minute challenge.

It doesn't matter what kind of plank we use. I prefer the pushup-position plank (PUPP), but any variation is fine. This two-minute test—and, yes, to quote one athlete I worked with, "it is arbitrary and mean-spirited"—challenges strength in all of its degrees and tests a bit of endurance.

What failure tells you is this: *The client is not strong enough.*

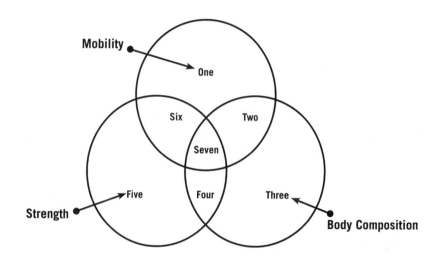

Using our Venn diagram, I look over at Section Five and see the client is a candidate for getting stronger—and please note, rarely is someone a pure *Five.*

One important thing to remember is that most NFL players and SEALs would be trained as *Sixes,* so don't think any of these categories are negative. We're just finding a starting position to begin to program what the person needs.

Many women are *Fours*; they can't hold the plank, and they have body-comp issues. Strength training, as many have discovered, is a superior way to achieve the lean body many women today aspire to have. The Cult of Cardio is slowly disappearing, and we find more and more women discovering the value of strength training.

Like the one-foot standing test, you may find your people practicing this test over and over. I can't imagine a better thing for your clients than to try to master the plank and the one-foot tests to, well, beat you.

Test Two: To the Floor and Back Up

The second test is a fundamental human movement. Sadly, in most gym settings we rarely see people getting on the floor, and this second assessment is so simple that you may completely miss the point. Follow these instructions: Sit down on the ground. Now stand up.

Fantastic—that's the whole test!

Claudio Gil Araújo, who performed a study at Clinimex-Exercise Medicine Clinic in Rio de Janeiro, said being able to stand up from a seated position on the ground was "remarkably predictive" of physical strength, flexibility and coordination at a range of ages.

Araújo said: "If a middle-aged or older man or woman can sit and rise from the floor using just one hand—or even better without the help of a hand—they are not only in the higher quartile of musculo-skeletal fitness, but their survival prognosis is probably better than that of those unable to do so."

Each of the two basic movements is assessed—to the ground, and then back to standing—and scored up to five, making a composite score of ten, with one point subtracted per support used, such as a hand or knee.

Here's the interesting part: Those who scored three points or fewer had a five to six times higher risk of death than those scoring more than eight points. A score below eight was linked with two to fivefold higher death rates over the 6.3-year study period.

Doctor Araújo again: "Our study also shows that maintaining high levels of body flexibility, muscle strength, power-to-body weight ratio and coordination are not only good for performing daily activities, but have a favorable influence on life expectancy."

Although this test is not specific to the Venn diagram, it's useful in providing a direction for programming. Improving this test may or may not be good for keeping the Angel of Death from the door, but it certainly brings more competence and safety to one's daily life.

Get Back Ups

One of the things I've realized is that many Americans literally spend no time on the ground. So, I came up with a little teaching drill that masquerades as a cardiovascular workout for some and a mobility workout for others.

It's called "Get Back Ups" or GBUps.

There's an important key to using this drill: *Do not overcoach.* In fact, intentionally undercoach the whole movement.

Announce the position on the ground—on the front, on the right side, on the left side, pushup-position plank or on the back. Wait for the client or clients to get in position. When all have stopped moving, announce, "Get back up."

When all are standing still, move to the next position.

Series One

The hands are free.

- On your front (or on your belly)
- Get back up
- On your right side
- Get back up
- On your left side
- Get back up
- Pushup-position plank
- Get back up
- On your back
- Get back up

Series Two

The right hand is stuck to the right knee (tell them a puppy dies if the hand comes loose from the knee).

- On your front (or on your belly)
- Get back up
- On your right side
- Get back up
- On your left side
- Get back up
- Pushup-position plank
- Get back up
- On your back
- Get back up

Series Three

The left hand is stuck to the left knee.

- On your front (or on your belly)

- Get back up
- On your right side
- Get back up
- On your left side
- Get back up
- Pushup-position plank
- Get back up
- On your back
- Get back up

Series Four

The right hand is stuck to the left knee.

- On your front (or on your belly)
- Get back up
- On your right side
- Get back up
- On your left side
- Get back up
- Pushup-position plank
- Get back up
- On your back
- Get back up

Series Five

The left hand is stuck to the right knee.

- On your front (or on your belly)
- Get back up
- On your right side
- Get back up
- On your left side

- Get back up
- Pushup-position plank
- Get back up
- On your back
- Get back up

I use the phrases, "Both hands in the back pocket," "Hands behind the head," and "Hands on shoulders" for variety.

The PUPP stays in the rotation regardless of hand position, and it's enlightening to see how people attempt to do these.

Doing all five series is a total of twenty-five reps of going up and down, and the group will be hot and sweating. It's a fine warmup, but it also seems to improve movement. As the movements are restricted when we put a hand on a knee, people need to come up with new strategies to get down and back up.

Doing these series, whether all of them or just some of them, improves the score on the Araújo test. Elderly clients seem to learn to simplify the movements and cut out the extra steps up and down. The feet become planted, and there's a drive upward with the whole leg and glutes.

We're cheating the test, certainly, but there's great value in increasing the amount of time that clients spend standing up from and sitting down on the floor.

A final tip here: A program that combines swings or squats with a pushup will get your clients successfully on and off the ground. If you mix and match things well, it will become dance-like in its flow. This kind of program should result in some changes in the overall assessment.

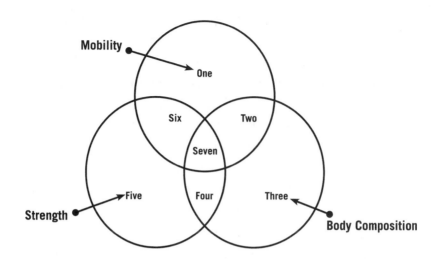

Test Three: Standing Long Jump

The third test—and again, this is optional for many clients—is the classic standing long jump. The goal is simple: The client must jump over body height. Not vertically… Horizontally! This is the standing long jump.

Using the measurement from the height-to-waist test (I told you height was important), either draw a line as a goal to get over, or just have the client jump, and then mark and measure.

Jumping less than height is an issue. Is it a lack of power or a lack of mobility? Either way, after training awhile, achieving this worthy goal will indicate that the training program is on the right path.

One of the first articles I ever read on the internet (we call them "blogs" now) was about jumping and quick lifts. The author, Clarence Bass, began with this story—

"Do you do any jumping?" asked Dr. Terry Todd, Co-Editor (with wife Jan) of *Iron Game History* and keeper of the Todd-McLean physical culture collection at the University of Texas, Austin. Talking to Terry is always fun and informative; he's in touch with just about everybody connected with the weight sports. Terry—a big man who weighed over 300 pounds in his heyday as a champion lifter—regaled me with the story of how he used to win tavern bets by jumping flat-footed up on bar counters. Turning serious, he related that, approaching 60 years of age, he still includes jumping and fast lifting movements in his training. "You know," he explained, "people lose the spring in their legs when they get older; I've seen old people who literally cannot jump up on a curb." Obviously, Terry doesn't intend to let that happen to him.

The loss of explosive movement, a "spring," is one of the markers of old age. Although we want to be safe and not cause injury in training, we must find ways to maintain and then build upon current levels of overall explosion with our older clients. The ability to pop is connected to the appearance of the glutes; again, the butt is the key to a youthful appearance and the secret to youthful power.

For the elite athlete, we expect more than body height. If everyone in a specific sport does standing long jumps (SLJs) over nine feet, that's the target for an elite athlete in that sport. A coach could say, "Somewhere between six feet and nine feet is your problem right now," and insist on more power, strength and mobility training.

If training increases the SLJ, things are going well. If training decreases the long jump, I think you have a problem. The SLJ measures explosive power and overall joint health. Keep an eye on decreases in jumping and address them quickly. Retest the height-to-waist measurement and reassess bodyweight if the SLJ numbers drop.

Test Four: Farmer Walk

The fourth and final test changed my career: the farmer walk. It was the missing ingredient of my training, and once I added it I began a new start as a thrower. In my forties, I threw farther than in my thirties, and the only change, beyond two daughters, tuition payments, a mortgage and two pets, was the farmer walks.

The farmer walk assesses overall work capacity. Let me just say right here that it's hard to measure work capacity.

Some tests are flawed, like testing professional basketball players on indoor cycles to find VO_2 max. Many basketball players can't fit on a normal bike, and others have never bicycled—obviously their scores will suffer.

Years ago some coaches tested physical conditioning with a one-mile run. I certainly understand why, but at the same time, the best miler would show the best results, which doesn't mean he'd be able to play offensive tackle or throw the shot put far.

The farmer walk assesses work capacity without the issues of most tests.

Farmer walking can be mastered in less than a minute, and the challenge to a person's grip, posture and overall conditioning is apparent on the first try. The test essentially boils down to this: Have your client do a farmer walk for a specific distance.

A few weeks later, after intelligent training, retest the movement. If the person goes farther, well, the training is increasing work capacity. If not, why not?

Load in the farmer walk has been the topic of a lot of serious discussion in our gym. Sophomore girls in high school can use eighty-five pounds per hand, yet this is well over bodyweight total. Some have argued for bodyweight in each hand, others half of bodyweight per hand. That's a big difference.

Still, as long as the load is the same for the before and after tests, it should be okay.

The downside is that people can go a long way…a loooong way…with too light a load. Most people using this test have discovered that erring on the side of weights being too heavy seems to work better.

Mike Warren Brown pointed out that so many people have issues trying to get a handle on loads in the farmer walk. We came up with a reasonable answer: Use the standards from the squat numbers in my book *Mass Made Simple* for individual people, and the trap bar numbers for gym members or large groups or teams.

Farmer Walk (*Mass Made Simple* Squat Standards)
Bodyweight on the left, load on the right

- Under 135 pounds: 135 pounds

- 136–185 pounds: 185 pounds

- 186–205 pounds: 205 pounds

- Over 206 pounds: 225 pounds

We experimented with half of bodyweight per hand using actual farmer bars, and it worked well, but that's not universally repeatable since many people don't have the specialty bars.

Kettlebells work well, too, and more people have those. Strive for bodyweight (half in each hand), but be aware that many places don't have enough bells at that weight.

Kettlebells (One in Each Hand)
Bodyweight on the left, load on the right

- Under 135 pounds: Double 24s

- 136–185 pounds: Double 32s

- 186–216 pounds: Double 40s

- Over 216 pounds: Double 48s

Always stay with the same loading, with one exception: growing young athletes. They might need to jump up in load year to year as they grow in size during puberty. I started high school at 118 pounds and grew to 162 as a senior. Then, I started Olympic lifting and grew to 218 pounds…100 pounds heavier in four calendar years. I obviously would have needed a heavier load as I grew.

Recapping the Tests
These four tests can also be a performance program. The plank, the GBUps, the standing long jump and the farmer walk test a number of important qualities, but are also self-measurable. Clients and athletes can practice and improve on these tests.

Moreover, these tests also reflect the needs of life and living. People want to be able to recover from a fall, leap over a rattlesnake and carry packages a long way. They want to have a core worthy of all the bends and twists of life.

Can You Go?

It takes some time to finish all of these physical tests, and many clients will be unable to perform some of the challenges. That's fine. It can be an excellent goal, long term, to be able to efficiently and effectively do all of the movements.

Chapter 4

Grade the Mirror: Assessing the Program

The Hidden Value

There is a hidden value in the four tests. They allow the coach and trainer to assess not just the person, but the program.

Assessments are so intertwined with goal setting that the best way to think about goals and assessments is as a figure eight, where goals and assessments run in a continual loop. Setting goals points us in the right direction, assessments feed the process with updated goals, and off we go in a loop of goal and assessment, goal and assessment.

However, there's a gap in most assessments. Usually, we assess the athlete, client, person or student. And then a few weeks later, we reassess. That sounds right, yes?

What we forget to assess is the training program we put this person on!

And that's the key. I'm not sure why this obvious point is so often overlooked, but we must assess the program as well as the person.

There are bad programs. There are bad DVD workouts. There are bad methods of training. How do we separate the wheat from the chaff? Assess them and find out!

Lewis Caralla, a young strength coach, and I were talking about this vital point.

"Grade the mirror," he muttered.

"What was that?"

"Grade the mirror," he responded, a little louder this time.

That's it. All too often, we throw a bunch of exercises, sets and reps and workout goo into a blender, press the puree button and call it a training program. Then we gobble it down.

Any new training idea might be great, but let's grade the mirror. Let's assess both the person and the program.

I grade the mirror with two tests we've used before: the standing long jump (SLJ) and the farmer walk (FW). If both the jump and the walk improve after a program or a new exercise or idea, I can be fairly confident it was a good thing.

If the FW improves and the SLJ drops, I need to look at what we gave up. If the SLJ improves and the FW drops, that might be okay for a power athlete, but a problem for someone who needs a higher level of conditioning. If both drop…we have a problem.

So, grade the mirror and assess the programming every so often.

Answering the Most Common Questions about the 1-2-3-4 Assessment

The Pillow Question

Q. I sleep on my side with a pillow between my knees to keep my hips level. I think that's safer than spending eight hours with one leg angled down. This might be common among women. Am I still a mobility client?

A. The pillow question is a fun one. No one has ever given me a false answer, as there's no stigma to it. If I ask if people buckle a seat belt, few would answer, "No!," as common sense and research practically forces us to answer, "Yes," no matter what we actually do in life.

The pillow question, as we see by the question above, opens a door. Many of us might use extra pillows from habit or comfort or just keeping the dog's breath farther away from our face.

For the assessor, it also prompts us to ask about mobility work, flexibility training and the key to recovery, which of course is sleep.

If a person puts a pillow here or there for this reason or that, it's fine. As we begin to plan out a training program, we're going to be sure to actively include mobility work throughout the training. I can't think of a person who doesn't need to access and appreciate a full range of motion throughout every joint in the body.

As I type, my neck stiffens up from injuries from playing football. Old wrist injuries make me roll my wrist joint around and do a few finger movements. Most adults I know have similar issues. As I often tell people, "Don't worry if you don't have mobility issues today. You probably will soon."

Can You Go?

Something like the Functional Movement Screen (FMS) or various other mobility tests can be a great next step in evaluation. Our job with the *1-2-3-4 Assessment* is to find a place to start when programming a person's first workout.

After a hard workout of hinges and squats, your client still might find the need for additional pillows.

Ongoing Assessments

Q. Do you just do the same *1-2-3-4 Assessment* every two weeks?

A: You certainly could, but you don't have to. I like to test something about every two weeks. It can be as simple as a mobility test like one of the seven tests from the FMS, or sometimes we revisit the plank or waist measurement.

You can organize this, if you like, so that every three months or so, you do each mobility test once or twice, and do a full screen once. You can easily test pullups, pushups and a variety of strength movements just about any time.

The key is recording these test results and watching for improvement.

The 300-Pound Question

Q: Your 300-pound weight line, is it lower for women?

A. My doctor was clear about this: Man or woman, the line in the sand is 300 pounds.

I certainly have no issue with sending each and every client off to the eye doctor, dentist and medical doctor, but I insist upon it if they're over 300 pounds.

But I know this: If you decide that *every* client walking through the door must get these medical exams, you probably won't have any clients. They'll listen to daytime television doctors, the lady at the salon and the guy next to them on the airplane, but getting them to make and show up to a medical appointment is a challenge.

When I first came on the internet, I stumbled upon a group of women who called themselves "The 100-Pound Club." To join the group, you had to lose 100 pounds. I found the group very welcoming, and I basically listened and learned from their experiences. Their process was usually a series of simple steps all of us would recognize: more water intake, some lifting, drastically cutting carbs and watching for food triggers.

There were a lot of health problems discussed in the group forum threads. A lot of medical advice was given to the newbies from people who had lost a lot of weight, but had never darkened the door of a medical school.

I'm fine with erring on the side of caution with any client. But, ask twenty people the following question: "Have you been to the eye doctor, the dentist and a medical doctor in the past year?" You'll be amazed at how few answer, "Yes."

So, insist on medical assessment for those over 300 pounds, and encourage everyone else to maintain an active medical history.

How to Evaluate Test Success

Q. What if the person "passes" all three of the tests?

A. The person who has the waistline at or under the 2:1 ratio, sleeps with only one pillow and can handle the plank for two minutes is doing well. In my times assessing Americans, I don't honestly see many of these.

I would suggest training them like a *Six* in the Venn diagram.

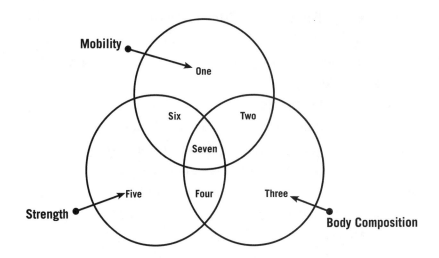

Mobility and strength work are always good for the human body. In addition, I would encourage them to participate in some kind of active hobby, and perhaps athletics.

Rock climbing will remind people to keep the bodyweight in check far better than a daily hop on the bathroom scale. They'll feel those extra pounds as they pull their bodyweight higher.

Anything people can do to embrace an active lifestyle and continue to move will pay benefits in the future.

Purpose of Assessing

Q. What does this assessment do for me? What's next?

A. The assessment process gives the coach and trainer a clear road map for the next three to nine sessions. Remember, we're discovering what people *need,* not what they want. Our job is to get them to turn their rudder in another direction. The assessment shows us which way to go; it tells us what needs to be done.

We want them to stay on the path toward the goal.

Chapter 5

The General Application of the 1-2-3-4 Assessment

Using the Assessment

Let's start our discussion of how to use the assessment with the person who doesn't fit anywhere on the Venn diagram. This could be someone who doesn't have any issues...right now!

Those of us who have issues are thinking, "Well, good for you, but time will tell."

Even if a client sleeps with one pillow, has an ideal waistline and can hold a plank for the month of July, we'd still like to train and practice. As a side note, I train off-season professional athletes—often *Sixes*—almost exactly like this, too.

Basically, try to blend all the fundamental human movements with mobility moves, and strive to keep moving. If you train

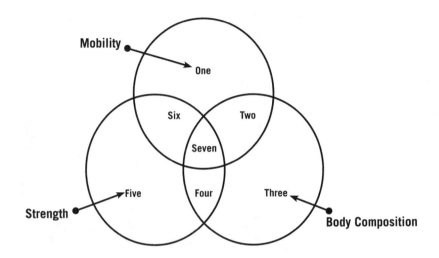

everything with very little rest between movements—a concept we call seamless training—your client's heart rate will impress even our cardio-focused friends.

But applying an overriding philosophy of strength training has to be put into bite-sized pieces. How do you organize it? How do you control it? Moreover, how do you address the daily training session in light of the weekly session, with an eye on the lifetime goals of the trainee?

The answer is obvious to most of us: We need to step back and look at the big picture of the life of the trainee, and settle on the direction to accomplish the goal. From there, we can drive it narrower, into perhaps a year-long approach, and from there sneak into the weekly and daily perspectives.

The word "fractals" comes to mind. A fractal is a never-ending pattern. Fractal patterns are extremely familiar, since nature is full of them—trees, rivers, coastlines, mountains, clouds, seashells and hurricanes, just to name a few. A leaf resembles a tree; a small stone looks like a mountain. If done correctly, a training day can look like a career.

Jurassic Park offers us an interesting counterpoint, or perhaps it's a warning—

> And that's how things are. A day is like a whole life. You start out doing one thing, but end up doing something else, plan to run an errand, but never get there... And at the end of your life, your whole existence has the same haphazard quality, too. Your whole life has the same shape as a single day.

I prefer to plan my clients' daily programs with the big picture in mind, based on these three simple principles—

1. Focus on movements, not muscles: The fundamental human movements are push, pull, hinge, squat, loaded carries and the sixth movement. The "sixth movement" is everything else we can do in training. Groundwork and tumbling are excellent examples.

2. Do it every day. In the words of Dan Gable, "If it's important, do it every day. If it isn't, don't do it at all."

3. Repeat, repeat, repeat. To tie it all together, do these fundamental human movements every day, and with lots of repetitions.

Even in all the movements, remember that enough is enough. More is often too much, and missing this concept gets a lot of people in trouble.

Now, if someone wants to be the best, we need to test against the highest and tightest standards. I often think back to an amazing story from Stephen Sondheim, the great songwriter and Broadway legend—

> *When I was fifteen, I wrote a show for George School, the Friends school I went to. It was called "By George," and was about the students and the faculty. I was convinced that Rodgers and Hammerstein couldn't wait to produce it, so I gave it to Oscar (Hammerstein) and asked him to read it as if he didn't know me. I went to bed dreaming of my name in lights on Broadway, and when I was summoned to his house the next day he asked, "Do you really want me to treat this as if I didn't know you?"*
>
> *"Oh yes," I said, to which he replied, "In that case, it's the worst thing I've ever read." He saw me blanch and continued, "I didn't say it was untalented, but let's look at it."*
>
> *He proceeded to discuss it as if it were a serious piece. He started right from the first stage direction; and I've often said, at the risk of hyperbole, that I probably learned more about writing songs that afternoon than I learned the rest of my life. He taught me how to structure a song, what a character was, what a scene was; he taught me how to tell a story, how not to tell a story, how to make stage directions practical.*

A good coach or mentor has the skill set to say, "This is the worst thing I have ever seen."

But, you can't stop there. You then have to point clients toward the path to success. This is the value of standards: A person seeking a goal needs to know the direction to take to get to the goal.

And on the flip side, if high standards have been achieved in the training hall, but the goals are not achieved on the field or on the bathroom scale, we can quickly turn to the other side of the performance model. Is the athlete doing enough intelligent practice or maintaining the fundamentals of the diet plan? As the personal training cliché goes, "you can't outwork a dozen doughnuts a day."

Writer Antoine de St. Exupery said, "In anything at all, perfection is finally attained not when there is no longer anything to add, but when there is no longer anything to take away, when a body has been stripped down to its nakedness."

The first step toward this is movement, then appropriate repetitions and, finally, load. Getting this order wrong leads to a lot of trouble, and nearly everything above can relate to each and every client, from the stiffest *One* to the most lost *Seven*.

Let's look at each category now.

The Threes: Diet and "Get Better"

Let's start with those in Section Three, the *Threes,* because this is where we'll find the bulk of the population. Moreover, this group will give us a chance to discuss appropriate dietary advice. Although it may seem confusing not to start with the *Ones*, it will make sense when you apply these methods. Basically, the bulk of the clients we deal with in fitness tend to need body composition work.

Addressing the *Threes* gives us an insight into both nutrition and fitness, and is relatively simple—

1. There must be some caloric restriction.

2. The person must do some inefficient exercise.

We could sum up all of the information for *Threes* like this—

- ♦ Cut out sugar.
- ♦ Cut out cardboard carbs.
- ♦ Get rid of Frankenstein fat.
- ♦ Eat colorful vegetables.
- ♦ Do something you're not good at, and get better at it. Then start over.

The diet and "get better" information is material that will nicely fill a lifetime. And this is pretty good advice for all seven subgroups.

The Fives: Lift Weights to Get Stronger

Let's jump to the *Fives*. As a strength coach, I find this section an easy one. I have a pretty simple formula for getting stronger, and I'm proud to have it survive over the nearly fifty years of my training career.

To get stronger, lift weights.

There, I said it.

I'm going to suggest a focus on the fundamental human movements—push, pull, hinge, squat, loaded carry and the sixth movement—that we'll cover in detail. Ideally, you should keep your *Five* client's total number of reps around fifteen to twenty-five, and increase the load when appropriate.

Trust me—as I'll explain later, if you can stick to the basic truths here, most people's strength deficits will be addressed quickly.

This does illuminate a point: *Add load to the push, pull, hinge, squat, loaded carry and the sixth movement, and keep the reps reasonable.*

That sentence was under twenty total words (and I waste words by not coming up with something more clever than "the sixth movement"), but the sentence will be true into the next millennia.

Of course, simply lifting all the books related to strength would be a fine workout. Just lift weights to get stronger, and don't get lost in the details.

The Fours: Strength Training for Body Comp

Many women will be *Fours*. I can't argue with Josh Hillis, my co-author of *Fat Loss Happens on Monday,* about the need for women to get stronger for their body composition goals. If you have the courage to use some logical caloric restriction and play with some inefficient exercise, *Fours* will find that getting stronger is the missing ingredient in the fat-loss recipe.

Josh notes that a woman who can do three dips, three pullups and five reps with 135 pounds in either the deadlift or the squat is "rock-star hot." I can't argue with him and his success, but to get some women to lift serious loads is difficult.

For inefficient exercise, I find the swing and pushup combination to be outstanding. Here are some examples from one of my training groups, the Coyote Point Kettlebell Club—

Workout Option One

- ◆ Swings for 20 seconds
- ◆ 6 pushups
- ◆ Rest for 30 seconds
- ◆ Repeat for 15 minutes

* Each workout, increase the pushups by one.

Workout Option Two

- ◆ 1 Pushup, then 1 Goblet Squat, then 10 Swings
- ◆ 2 Pushups, then 2 Goblet Squats, then 10 Swings

◆ 3 Pushups, then 3 Goblet Squats, then 10 Swings

◆ 4 Pushups, then 4 Goblet Squats, then 10 Swings

◆ 5 Pushups, then 5 Goblet Squats, then 10 Swings

The Ones: Mobility Work

A pure *One* might be a rarity: Someone who is clearly immobile is not common among the groups I've worked with. However, it's possible to do yoga four days a week and still have mobility issues.

Increasing flexibility is often a neurological trick. We're "turning off" certain muscles and hanging out on the connective tissues. Flexibility and mobility must always be framed around the word "enough." More flexibility is not necessary, except in some rare areas of dance and high-level gymnastics.

Enough is enough; more is not better.

I strongly suggest focusing on Janda's tonic muscles for flexibility work. Be sure the pectorals, biceps, hamstrings and hip flexors, as well as the adductor muscles of the thighs, are the focus. Mobilizing these muscles will do more to counterbalance life, sitting and commuting than two hours of general stretching.

As with strength work and caloric restriction, when it comes to mobility, enough is enough. More is not better.

The Twos: Fixing Either One Fixes the Two

Twos get an interesting bang for the buck. The more mobile they become, the less they tend to toss and turn at night. They don't hurt as much while they sleep, so they can stay in one place a bit more and not do an all-night tumbling routine.

And not tossing and turning all night will keep partners happier, too. Many of us know this eternal truth: A happier partner leads to a happier life.

I'm still convinced that one hundred years from now, part of the answer to the current obesity epidemic will have been answered by our failure to get enough sleep. Sleep more and lose body fat. Surely that's the *easiest* fat-loss advice your clients will ever hear!

The Sixes: Strength and Mobility

Sixes provide us with a template for training elite athletes and those involved in collision occupations. In the off-season of any professional athlete, we just mix strength movements with mobility work. Rest periods are the mobility training.

For strength training, focus on Janda's phasic muscles: the glutes, deltoids, triceps and ab wall. Corrective work outside of basic mobility—foam rolling, ball rolling, band work or whatever—should also be done between strength training sets.

By using a heart rate (HR) monitor, you can gain insights into cardiovascular work. This style of training—mixing strength with mobility and correctives—can keep your client's HR in a training zone of cardiovascular conditioning. In other words, this method gives the benefits of jogging while increasing strength and flexibility.

In the last section of the book (see page 187), I'll show you *Hypertrophy and Mobility,* an interesting way to train advanced athletes and those who are *Sixes.*

Sevens: Everything Works

Sevens are wonderful. Anything we can get them to do is going to work, and all we need is some level of commitment. This can be as simple as getting them to commit to drinking two cups of water a day.

Don't be surprised if you get responses such as, "Wow, that's a *lot*." A friend of mine started off his one-hundred-pound weight loss (in one year!) by committing to drink two glasses of water a day for a month. For much of the first two weeks, he accomplished this task at ten o'clock at night because he couldn't get around to it until then.

A year later, though, he was a hundred pounds lighter.

Successfully accomplishing the easier tasks creates a mind-set for future success. Rather than trying to seek perfection during the first month, seek success over the long term—and help your clients do the same.

Everything and anything works: Master the basics, move better and move more.

I know you can do more. I know your client can do more. I know everybody can do more. I would argue, however, that you should keep things simple and basic for as long as you can—for both yourself and for your clients.

Seek mastery.

Then, every few weeks, reassess.

Fewer pillows, a smaller waistline and more time in the plank are always good and noteworthy. If your client's standing long jump and farmer walk have improved, you know your program is working. Keep doing it.

For most of us, whether we're *Ones, Twos, Threes, Fours, Fives, Sixes, Sevens* or anything else, it comes down to this—

- Stretch what is tightening—pecs, biceps, hip flexors, hamstrings.

- Strengthen what is weakening—glutes, abs, delts, triceps.

- Eat like an adult.

- Seek mastery.

If there was a secret to programming for most people, we'd find this—

1. As we learned from Gray Cook, we should aspire to move without pain, to move well and to move often.

2. Intelligent, repeatable workouts over years trump injuries and surgeries.

3. Recovery is when adaption occurs, so plan it into your programs.

As someone told me a few years ago, the key is to "live long and well, then drop dead."

Chapter 6

The Five Tools

A Glance at the Tools

The five focuses outlined earlier form the basis of training programs for all seven QIII E^2 "everybody else" subgroups and are what I call the *Five Tools—*

1. Nutrition and caloric restriction

2. Inefficient exercise

3. Strength training

4. Hypertrophy and mobility training—the Fountain of Youth

5. Mental set

After the *1-2-3-4 Assessment,* you'll know if a particular client is a *One, Two, Three, Four, Five, Six* or *Seven.*

Remember, if the person is an active athlete, your job is to support the technical work with a reasonable program focused on the fundamental human movements.

In addition, if someone doesn't fit into one of the seven categories but is *not* an active athlete, train the person as a *Six*.

We are going to now focus on the *Five Tools* as ways to help your clients feel better, move better and, ideally, live better. Each of the *Five Tools* is interconnected, and each can be confusing and frustrating for everyone from the researcher to the mom choosing dinner while her two hungry kids are fidgeting in the shopping cart. With each, forget about perfection and begin the process of moving forward to a generally "good place."

The first tool, nutrition and caloric restriction, tends to be a touchy subject. No matter what I discuss concerning nutrition, I usually upset someone. Still, our approach, honed by regular discussions with nutritionists, is solid advice that I believe will stand the test of time.

The middle three tools—inefficient exercise, strength, hypertrophy and mobility training—involve movement of all kinds.

Try to get a handle on the idea that equipment is simply a tool; it's how you use the tool that matters. One person's inefficient exercise might be another's mobility movement. And that's fine.

The final tool is the mind, and here we tend to work best in extremes. Either option offered in that section may work for your clients.

The First Tool: Nutrition and Caloric Restriction

Caloric restriction involves talking about nutrition, and nutrition is going to lead to discussing food.

I don't know if there's anything as confusing as something so simple as what to shove in your mouth a few times a day. Whether or not a food is good for us is enough to cause fistfights. Recently, all of the following have been outed as being bad for us—

- Coffee (Hearing this made me spit out my coffee!)

- Wine (What else does one serve with veggies?)

- Vegetables (Too many pesticides! Wine and coffee don't have those…I think.)

- Tap Water (Poisons and heavy metals!)

- Meat (For a while in the 1960s, eating meat was on par with launching nuclear weapons.)

- Milk (From "producing mucus" to "lactose intolerant")

- Grains (I heard one speaker call this "public enemy number one.")

It seems that few of us know what to eat. Yet we all bravely carry on eating. I can't keep up with all the conflicting information, and most other people seem to struggle with it too.

At our gym, we attempt to tell the story of reasonable eating and reasonable fitness. We strive to keep a moderate and balanced approach to all goals.

The problem is this: Most people don't hear us.

Bill Koch, an American world champion in cross-country skiing, did a workshop years ago in Salt Lake City. For ten dollars, I figured eight hours with a world champ and Olympic medalist was a bargain.

There was a problem with the workshop: I still feel like I was the only participant who could hear him. It seemed the audience wanted elaborate programming, fancy training equipment and expensive gear. His answers were always simple and clear.

"Intervals are the biggest bang for your buck."

"My daughters take the lift up the hill; I ski up it and race them down."

But the workshop still ended up being a series of intricate questions about the smallest details of training, and Koch's response was always, "No, I don't do that."

The audience couldn't hear what he was saying. It's a problem we see in every field: Most people want to be reaffirmed about their current methods of doing things.

When people ask, "What's the best diet?," what do they want to hear? I think it's, "The one you're on."

As we joke around our gym, the best diet most people will ever do is the *next* one.

So, what's best? Atkins? Zone? Vegan? Paleo? I'm not sure which is best, but I know that the adherents of some diets might physically attack you for eating the wrong kind of food.

"Don't you know that X is poison, and your children will suffer tragically if they go near it?"

That's hyperbole, but closer to reality than most people will admit.

So, which is the best diet? My standpoint shouldn't surprise anyone at this point, but I believe they're *all* right. There's a joke about Jesus and the miracle of the loaves and fish. As his disciples are handing out the free food, the audience starts yelling back.

"Is the fish mercury tested?"

"Is the bread gluten free?"

"I'm a vegan!"

If you want to have a fun plane ride, sit between a vegan and a Paleo. The standard line is this: "How do you know someone's a vegan? You met her five minutes ago. How do you know someone is a CrossFitter? You met him ten seconds ago."

There are some people who follow strict diets with the religious fervor of a convert, the discipline of a monk and the know-it-allness of a teenager.

Let's be big kids with food. Yes, fast food is bad and made from asphalt, toxic sewage and road kill. Or whatever.

Beyond that, what I look for are the consistent truths. What do all the ways of eating agree upon for daily consumption and daily avoidance?

I've found five truths that practically every way of eating agrees upon—

1. Cut back on sugar.

2. Cut out cardboard carbs.

3. Get rid of Frankenstein fats.

4. Eat colorful vegetables.

5. Let's all find what to agree on before we seek perfection.

Although some argue sugar consumption hasn't increased as much as originally thought, we still consume too much. Overall, our kids eat too much sugar—we need to make them stop that. I've looked, and I can't find one good argument for eating more sugar or maintaining the amount of sugar we're currently eating. Cut out sugar.

Cardboard carbs are any carbohydrate found in a bag or box. If it can last on your shelf for ten years, it will remain on your butt that long, too. Cut them out.

Given a cow and a video on how to make butter, I can make butter. But give me corn, and I can't squeeze margarine out of it. It takes a lab. It takes equipment. It takes a scientist. Mother Nature doesn't seem to be able to figure out how to deal with these Frankenstein fats, and neither can the human body. Get rid of them.

Every diet agrees on the value of colorful vegetables. Those green, yellow, orange and red veggies will do wonders for you. Eat them.

The point is this: Let's get to where all of the various ways of eating agree. I'm not sure the perfect diet exists, and if it did, the body would figure out a way around that, too.

Let's instead keep focused on eating pretty good and forget perfect. I've said it before, in my book *Mass Made Simple*—

> Eat like an adult. Stop eating fast food, stop eating kid's cereal, knock it off with all the sweets and comfort foods whenever your favorite show is not on when you want it on. Ease up on the snacking and—don't act like you don't know this—eat more vegetables and fruits.

And in my workshops, I often add this little list for simple nutritional advice—

- Eat like an adult!
- Eat vegetables.
- Eat lean protein.
- Drink water.
- Train in a fasted state—sometimes.
- Stay hungry after training—sometimes.

Recently, a hand came up after my comment about training in a fasted state. The person wanted to know if I followed this "modern" intermittent fasting idea. Fortunately, I had a slide prepared—

"Obese people and those desiring to lose weight should perform hard work before food. Meals should be taken after exertion while still panting from fatigue. They should, moreover, only eat once per day and take no baths and walk naked as long as possible."

~ Hippocrates, circa 471 BC

Hippocrates was recommending intermittent fasting long before the internet or bound books. I'm not as sure about the bathing and nudity points, but I can defend the first sentence without much issue.

Over a century ago, Herbert Shelton notes in *The Hygienic System*, "The ancient Greeks—the finest of people, physically and mentally, that ever lived—ate but two meals a day."

By the way, not eating is a common way to approach caloric restriction. In the religious traditions, this is called fasting, and there are a lot of degrees here, from simple hunger to dangerous starvation.

Pavel Tsatsouline summed up the whole diet question for athletes like this: "Meat for strength. Veggies for health."

Marc Halpern, my resident nutritionist, captures the essence of nutrition for us with a straightforward arrow.

...as you move to the right...

Pizza and Candy　　　　　　　　　　　**Vegetables, Meat & Fruit**

Move to the right as far as you need.
Your perfect place is a blend of
health, lifestyle and values.

Out there on the far right, at the tip of the arrow, is diet perfection. Forget it. Choose more salads and vegetables, but don't try to be faultless. When it comes to diet and nutrition, especially in terms of caloric restriction, doing more, better, is where things work best.

Less candy. More veggies.

The Second Tool: Inefficient Exercise

On the other side of the fat-loss coin is the concept that everything works and it always has. Whatever you choose to do or have your clients do—whether it's African disco dance or step-marching in Spandex or kettlebell swings—it will work.

The problem is a little odd: As we become more and more efficient, we get less and less fat-loss benefit. A modern dance class will just about kill me, because every time the class does "step-ball-change," I will have done twenty extra moves. Oh, it will be fat loss for me—but the twinkle toes to my right had better have a perfect diet, because when we're dancing, she's just going through the paces.

Fat-loss exercise needs to be as inefficient as possible. That's why I like the kettlebell swing: We expend tons of energy with absolutely no movement! But, and many disagree with me here, as we get better and better at swings, these can also become too efficient.

We have tips and tools to get around this, but it's wise to remember that Tim Ferriss found seventy-five swings, three days a week, to be enough to start peeling the fat off of one woman. If your client goes from seventy-five to two thousand swings a workout and stops losing fat, you may need to look for alternatives, additions or another bell.

Inefficient exercise will look different for everyone—if your client is a horrible dancer, encourage him to dance; if your client is a lousy swimmer, encourage her to swim; if your client never bikes, encourage him to bike.

For fat loss, we have to seek ways to waste lots of energy. Leonard Schwartz had it right with his HeavyHands training. Tossing hand weights up and down while walking is a very poor way to walk—but it sure roasts off the fat!

And, I know, you can't hear me. A reasonable approach to diet and nutrition, something your grandmother would applaud, just isn't sexy enough for the postmodern reader.

The Third Tool: Strength Training

Assessment allows us to see that our clients are on the path to their goals. Now it's time to talk about the path. There are hundreds of options in training, but what's more important than the daily workout or yearly plan is the philosophy of training.

It takes a while to come to clarity on a philosophy of training. My approach continues to evolve and becomes more clear, although the principles have been around for a long time. My greatest insight came from a long-distance phone call with a friend, Mike Rosenberg.

I edited a fun little online newsletter called *Get Up!* for about a decade. In hindsight, its little run was amazing. We had reports from Olympic gold medalists who wanted to share their training ideas, programs of world-record holders, perhaps the first eyewitness report of how the Chinese were training the Olympic lifts and countless firsthand stories of "how I did it."

It was wonderful stuff, but the editing and writing was taking up a lot of my time. It died a quiet death, but the archives are still available on my site, *danjohn.net.* The price, we always said, is going to double next month. The joke: All the editions are free. Contain your laughter.

In the second edition, Rosenberg told me to include my philosophy of training. Mike and I discussed what it was, and we slowly fleshed out these three points—

1. The body is one piece.

2. There are three kinds of strength training: putting weight overhead, picking it up off the ground, and carrying it for time or distance.

3. All training is complementary.

Let's look at all of these in detail.

"The body is one piece" idea came from John Jerome's remarkable book, *Suppleness.* I often say you could add any superlative in front of "piece" to make the point better: The body is one *amazing* piece. The body is one *astonishing* piece. The body is one *stupendous* piece. I think you get the point. It means things like, if you have diarrhea, today is not a good day to squat heavy. If you're doing a chest exercise like the bench press and I stick your calf with a fork, you're going to be in trouble with a bar across your neck.

Sadly, most people still train like they're building Frankenstein's monster. Arm day. Leg day. Chest day.

The body is one piece, with one digestive tract, one cardiovascular system, and one magnificent nervous system. If your client has trouble "here," that person is going to have trouble "there." If the supply of blood to a client's brain is shut off, the training will be impaired.

That's not medical advice, by the way.

This first principle separates the good coaching from the less-than-stellar coaching. A college athlete walking into a workout after breaking up with the beloved is going to have a different workout than what the coach planned. Sure, it's just a mild case of a broken heart, but with a proper dynamic mobility warmup, I'm positive we can cure this!

Recovery needs to be planned, too. In my youth, I was told it took eight days to recover from an NFL game, but, sadly, they play every seven. To my knowledge, Bill Walsh was the first NFL coach to come to the idea that practice is, well, practice.

Your clients' days, weeks, kids, bosses and just about everything else will impact their training, for bad or good. Disease or illness will burden the system.

And let me offer you this: Idiotic training and programming will be as toxic to the system as many diseases. I've had my share of parasites in my life (sadly, true), and a good case or two of pleurisy, and these were easily overcome compared to idiocy and tomfoolery in the gym. One moment of too much load, poor technique or just bad timing can hold a person back for months, years or even decades. I've had friends strive to recover from muscles ripped off a bone, spinal injuries and a variety of broken bones and twisted and ripped joints.

Understanding that the body is one piece begins the process of seeing the life of the athlete, a training year and a workout from a more distant vantage point. It's a global view, a paradigm shift from seeing everything as bits and pieces like Frankenstein's monster to seeing everything as miraculously interconnected.

The second point is that there are three kinds of strength training. It's taken me twelve years to come up with a better way to explain this. Obviously, I still stand by it, but some good questions have come up. The best came up when the fitness leaders fell back in love with movement. This field falls in love with everything new, exciting and shiny, and, frankly, I fall on the opposite side of new, exciting and shiny.

I like things basic and simple.

My gym is basic and simple. It's also my garage. It's heavy with kettlebells, barbells, TRXs, and a mishmash of stuff that allows us to handle up to two-dozen people, and get some great training in a short period of time.

For recovery, I have a hot tub, a sauna and a very interesting electronic massage bed that does all the work for me. I also have plenty of food and emergency supplies from beer to bandages, depending on the need.

Our place attracts a great range of people. I train with a nutritionist and the elderly, with high school coaches and people with life-altering diseases. Everyone is welcome—and by everyone, I include elite Special Forces personnel and NFL and MLB players.

The upside of all of this are the great conversations. You get a glimpse into the wide world of elite performance, and you hear some funny things.

One of our regulars is a Major League Baseball player. One of the things he likes about training at our gym is that we don't have "eyewash." What's eyewash? It's all that pomp and circumstance and grandstanding and "look at me, look at me" that dominates most fitness facilities. Listen, it's a burpee; you don't need to film it for the historical record. That's eyewash.

Eyewash abounds in our field. We need to get back to the basics of getting people to move more and move better so they can move more and move better.

Jim Gaffigan, one of my favorite comedians, has this great insight into Mexican food—

> Mexican food's great, but it's essentially all the same ingredients, so there's a way you'd have to deal with all these stupid questions.
>
> "What is nachos?"
>
> "Nachos? It's tortilla with cheese, meat and vegetables."
>
> "Oh, well then what is a burrito?"
>
> "Tortilla with cheese, meat and vegetables."
>
> "Well, then what is a tostada?"
>
> "Tortilla with cheese, meat and vegetables."
>
> "Well then what i—"
>
> "Look, it's all the same s—t! Why don't you say a Spanish word and I'll bring you something."

I see training people the same way. You want to play in the NFL? Good, then we have to do pushes, pulls, hinges, squats and loaded carries, plus the *everything else* that's mostly groundwork.

And you? MLB? Ah, yes, that would be pushes, pulls, hinges, squats and loaded carries.

Do you see that nice fat-loss client over there? She seems to need, I don't know, let's say, pushes, pulls, hinges, squats and loaded carries, plus the *everything else* that's mostly groundwork.

Programming is that simple. We all have the same basic body and needs, and we have to have the courage to train the fundamentals—the basics—at least 80 percent of the time.

Sure, add some spice now and again, but focus on the basics.

As I was told by a truly great coach, Rick Bojak: "You need to have the courage not to get bored watching the basics."

That's the key.

Yes, I know our clients and athletes come with all these great ideas about how to train after watching twenty seconds on the internet or a TV commercial, but it's our responsibility to steer them back to the basics.

Let's practice.

Client: "I saw blah blah blah on the internet, and I really want to give it a try."

Inside your brain, "Eyewash. Eyewash."

Program like this: Tortilla with cheese, meat and vegetables. Stick with the basics for everybody—

- *Pushes*
- *Pulls*
- *Hinges*
- *Squats*
- *Loaded carries*
- *Everything else, mostly groundwork*

Honestly, if your clients do the fundamental human movements with appropriate repetitions and load, they'll be well on their way to almost any goal.

The third pillar in my philosophy is that all training is complementary. As I've noted to many trainers, there's an "e" in there, not an "i." It isn't complimentary like, "Well, you look very good today, my young trainee! Excellent to see, and I love what you're wearing."

Complementary is a bit different. We need to be able to tell the client, "The soccer game you just played worked perfectly on honing your sprinting skills," or "Yoga would be a great place to practice that joint mobility work you want for increasing your sprinting speed."

Understanding the concept that all training is complementary frees up a lot of time as you begin to realize the key to success in training and life: More is usually just more.

One of my favorite stories comes to mind here. Henry David Thoreau and Ralph Waldo Emerson are sitting around one day, talking about life, when Thoreau pauses.

"Yes?" asks Emerson, expectantly.

"Simplify, simplify," says Thoreau.

"You didn't need the second 'simplify,'" replies Emerson.

It's hard to remember this basic point sometimes. Training programs, exercise selection and nutritional tweaks bombard us nearly every time we jump on the internet or flip open a fitness magazine. We get deluged with "try this" and "do that."

How do we filter what works for us or for our clients? How do we discern what will or won't work?

Start by discovering your philosophy for training. What are the basic suppositions that drive your vision of training, health and fitness?

Once you know this, it's time to design a multiyear, yearly, seasonal or daily program—a training session—by focusing on these three things—

1. Focus on movements, not muscles. Ignore the idea of biceps, quads or arm days. Stop thinking your clients are Frankenstein's monster. Training the movements will build muscles, stretch the client back into alignment and bring back joint mobility.

2. Do what's important every day. Once we know the moves, how often should they be done? My suggestion: every day. With most athletes, the movements need to be repeated far more than most people think. At the elite levels of track and field and Olympic lifting, the total number of full movements needed is staggering.

3. Repetitions…lots of repetitions. I can't say it any better than what I learned from a hearing-impaired discus thrower I worked with a few years ago. He had become very good, and I asked him his secret. He took his right middle finger and twisted it over his right index finger and then slapped it into his left palm. In sign language, it means "repetition."

The Fourth Tool: Hypertrophy and Mobility Training (the Fountain of Youth)

Let's say you're a well-meaning trainer and you decide to take ninety-three-year-old Grandpa on the journey back to teen muscle.

So, we pick up Grandpa and take him into one of these new "back to the jungle" training programs. Gramps has been in a wheelchair for seven years after falling in church. Sign him up for tree climbing and leaping off boulders and all the rest, which I respect, but then press "refresh" on your brain. How do we get Gramps from the wheelchair into the wilderness?

That's the value of machines. For post-youth hypertrophy, it's hard to argue with how well machines work. For the record, I'm not talking about machines as the answer to all questions after a six-week study proves that Nautilus, or whatever, makes a difference.

One of my readers sent me this study about how stretching alone improves strength in untrained people. Frankly, everything works for six weeks!

So, I see some hands raised.

"Yes?"

"Um, Danny, don't you hate machine training?"

Alas.

Before you ask, "Aren't you the O-lifting, Highland Games, football guy?," well, yes, I am, but there's great value in just about every training system.

Moreover, the longer you stay in the game, the more astute the following point attributed to Aristotle becomes: "The more you know, the more you know you don't know."

I had this same point explained to me as a circle. Inside the circle is everything you know. The circle line is where you touch all the things you don't know. As you study something more and more, the more you realize you have so much more to learn.

The more I learn and study, the less sure I am about anything. The same idea is true when someone takes a weekend certification program and suddenly knows how to fix everything from cancer to MS, and knows everything there is to know about sports.

In case you're wondering: I don't think a weekend is long enough to achieve mastery in anything.

Yes, I love Olympic lifts and kettlebells, but we need to keep in mind that every tool works, every method works, and every principle works…at the right time.

A few sets of eight to ten reps with a few strength moves and a touch of stretching to top things off may be life changing for the elderly. Seriously, a few movements will make a huge difference. It can be that simple: a few lifts and a few stretches.

Mastering the movements, however, is going to be a journey.

On this journey, there will be some obstacles. We need a system for dealing with these issues, and at the heart of it we find this: Strength training for lean body mass and joint mobility work trumps everything else.

How much time should you spend on hypertrophy and joint mobility? The answer is easy: all the time you can spare. If the goal is to live well enough, as long as you can, don't overlook either one.

Years ago, Vladimir Janda began discussing the muscles necessary for posture. To simplify—yes, that's always a slippery slope—he separated muscles into two groups: tonic, which tend to shorten when tired (or old!), and phasic, which tend to weaken under stress (or age, I dare say).

Tonic Muscles (Shorten)	Phasic Muscles (Weaken)
Upper Trapezius	Rhomboids
Pectoralis Major	Mid-back
Biceps	Triceps
Pectoralis Minor	Gluteus Maximus
Psoas	Deep Abs
Piriformis	External Obliques
Hamstrings	Deltoids
Calf Muscles	

I usually explain it this way: If a tiger chased you up a tree, the muscles you use to hang onto the branch for a long time are tonic muscles. If you decided to chase a deer, you'd use your phasic muscles.

Sadly, most trainers work this backward. They tend to emphasize the mirror muscles like the pecs and biceps—with, say, bench presses and curls—and ignore the muscles that really are the muscles of youth.

Training with the fundamental human movements will do more for hypertrophy, mobility and function than a million isolation moves. Janda taught us this, and now we can see how the chart above and the fundamental human movement are interrelated—

- ◆ Push: Deltoids and Triceps
- ◆ Pull: Rhomboids
- ◆ Hinge: Butt
- ◆ Squat: Butt
- ◆ Loaded Carries: Butt

The movements you're ignoring are the things your clients need the most!

As you look at that list, you should be impressed by the number of times "butt" appears. Training the glutes intelligently may be the fountain of youth!

So, movements first. Then, load.

We'll talk about reps, sets and load in more detail after we discuss the fifth tool.

The Fifth Tool: The Mental Set

My issue with both the fitness industry and most people's approaches to fitness and health is this: We want the quick, the fast, the overnight, the instant and the miracle. But how often does that really work? And when it doesn't work, how do we achieve those things that we want?

I have some difficult answers.

First, you *know* what to do, honestly. Your clients know what to do. Your mom knows. Lose weight? "Eat less, move more." Get stronger? "Lift weights." Get more mobile? "Move around a bit more, and move more appropriately."

Everyone knows the basics of what they need to know about health, fitness and longevity.

Second, fear tactics, like those we saw in the antismoking campaign, seem virtually worthless, too. After the initial whack of fear tactics, people tend to shrug them off over time.

Third, I'm a big fan of Tony Robbins and his system of incurring "instant" change. His work taught me as a coach what a big lever I have with pain. Pain motivates people better than any golden ring somewhere in the future. Personally, losing my ability to function normally to both illness and injury has provided more motivation than all the "win one for the Gipper" talks I ever heard.

If I can get elite athletes to think about the pain of failure, it seems to give them the motivation to continue to push forward. Honestly, though, I hate to pull this lever. It works, it's a valuable tool, but it diminishes the journey for all of us.

And for years, I didn't know a better way. Then I was told about making small changes.

We'll think about this mental aspect in more detail in the next chapter.

Chapter **7**

That Fifth Tool...For Most of Us

We're Not That Disciplined

Let's expand on the mental aspect of making small or "tiny" changes. Some people can do a 180 and turn their lives around in one smooth move. For most of us, though, we need to try another path; we need to improve our fitness and health one habit at a time.

I'm a big fan of the work of Josh Hillis in this area, but B. J. Fogg of Stanford University made me realize we need to make our habit changes even easier than I ever thought possible.

I'd love it if a client told me she was going to add eight different vegetables to her diet every day, but I doubt she would even get to the store. And if she did, she might find herself frustrated without the knowledge of what to do with all those veggies.

Let's make things easier—

- ◆ Commit to adding *one* vegetable a day.

- ♦ If buying canned veggies, only buy them with the pop-top lids. Saving that extra work of opening the can with a can opener makes a bigger difference than you'd think.

- ♦ Buy the precut, prewashed veggies. Yes, they're more expensive, but they're much easier to just drop into eggs, soups or stews without a second thought.

You want your client to drink more water? Get him to convince himself that for every cup of coffee or adult beverage he has, he'll have a sip of water. And remind him to congratulate himself after!

Why a sip, and not a glass of water?

Good question. I know this: I can always have a sip of water. I just rinse out the mug, splash a little extra in my mouth, think "Yes!" loudly to myself and carry on. To some, turning that sip into a glass changes the task from possible to impossible.

Here's the funny thing: Most of us think we're walking hulks of discipline. Actually, we're just masses of habits.

In high school, we had sixth-period PE, and all the athletes went to varsity practice. At 1:30 p.m., a mass of the school population headed over to the locker rooms.

It wasn't my self-discipline marching off to war; I was caught up in the current of people going to practice. For most of us, the day high school ended, so did our training. Fortunately, I was in the habit of training in my backyard. Later I got caught up in my college track team and the Pacific Barbell Club training schedule.

Years after that, with two kids, a dog and a cat and a mortgage, I came home every night and I sat down to ease my feet and watch TV. But, it was time to train!

I could actually hear my inner high school voice yelling out to me, "Hey, it's time to train!"

Simple to write, simple to say and simple to follow—but few people adhere to fitness programs for the central reason that they just *fail to show up.*

Even if people go to the gym or walk over to their fitness equipment with the intention of waving a few things around for thirty seconds, they're doing better than staying on the couch, bed or computer chair. Trust me, when we just show up, we'll do more than just a few waves.

Twyla Tharp said it best in her book, *The Creative Habit*—

> I begin each day of my life with a ritual; I wake up at 5:30 a.m., put on my workout clothes, my leg warm-ers, my sweatshirts, and my hat. I walk outside my Manhattan home, hail a taxi, and tell the driver to take me to the Pumping Iron gym at 91st Street and First Avenue, where I work out for two hours. The ritual is not the stretching and weight training I put my body through each morning at the gym; the ritual is the cab. The moment I tell the driver where to go I have completed the ritual.

> It's a simple act, but doing it the same way each morning habitualizes it—makes it repeatable, easy to do. It reduces the chance that I would skip it or do it differently. It is one more item in my arsenal of routines, and one less thing to think about.

Then, they must finish the program. No matter what you have clients do, whether it's two weeks to bigger biceps or six weeks to ripped abs, they have to finish the program.

Do not criticize, condemn or correct a training program a client is doing until it's complete—and encourage the client not to do so either.

Years ago, I followed a strict and disciplined diet that involved only protein shakes and twenty-eight days of hard living for everyone around me. Upon completion, a friend told me, "Now that you've finished it, you can criticize it."

That insight was so simple and clear, I now use it as a tool: Finish it; then fix it.

Follow the Trail

A while back, I put together a 10,000 swing challenge featuring two training programs for two different tasks. I undertook this challenge twice to figure out which rep schemes worked best over the course of the entire twenty-day program.

Within minutes of publishing the article outlining the challenge, I began receiving emails and posts with "better" ideas.

"Wouldn't it be better to do twenty sets of twenty-five reps to get five hundred a day?"

No, because you can never keep track of the sets. We tried it, and you simply get lost after a dozen sets.

"Wouldn't this rep scheme be better (insert a bunch of random numbers)?"

No, you see…and then I realized something: These people were asking questions without even trying the 10,000 reps. On day one of the article's publication, the readers were already coming up with "better" ideas without doing a single swing.

It reminded me of something my brother-in-law, Craig Hemingway, told me. He works as an EMT and often gives presentations to schools. He has a rule for every question-and-answer period: When you raise your hand, I want a question. A question finishes with a question mark. A story, on the other hand, is when you tell us about how your grandpa has been in an ambulance. We only want questions right now.

You see, most people want to tell their stories. They don't really want to follow my programs or anybody else's programs; they want to tell me about their programs.

Reflect on this quote by Amelia Earhart: "In soloing, as in other activities, it is far easier to start something than it is to finish it."

For nearly every single goal you have in mind, someone else has cleared the path before you. Why not just follow the trail?

When I try to explain group coaching in a workshop, often we have a few minutes of confusion. I've come up with a simple explanation: If you're training yourself, you'll tend to know everything you decide to do. You'll always push yourself exactly as hard as you feel like pushing yourself. You won't have any gaps in your training because you have no idea what you're lacking. Finally, you'll be able to progress and regress easily in your system since your single follower—you—will know what you want, even if it isn't something you need to do.

I hope I painted a picture of mediocrity here.

If you teach 10,000 people at once, you had better have a clear foundation, exacting progressions and regressions, nearly perfect instruction and several methods of instantly scaling the movement, the volume and the load.

Coaching a group of people takes having a larger system in place than does coaching yourself. As the number of athlete clients rises, the importance of clarity in your programming and coaching rises, too.

Here it is as a brilliant graph—

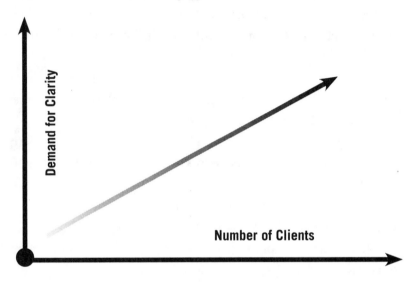

"No man is an island," said John Donne, and training on an island is going to be lonely and hard to find things like food, water and wifi. Training in community demands clarity, scalability and attention to detail. Training solo demands a lot of free will and self-discipline, something you might often find in short supply.

It's easy to harness the forces of will. How? By taking it from others!

To regather my self-discipline, I turned my free will over to something else: *intentional community*.

Intentional Community

I'm sure all of us have this issue some days: Sometimes, I have *no* interest in training. My gym, which serves the dual purpose of being a two-car garage, recently measured nine degrees Fahrenheit. Alice Lopez always gives us the gym temperature in

Celsius, and when she says it's "minus whatever," it doesn't make me excited to train.

Sometimes, I don't want to get up. I don't want to train.

But it doesn't matter. Why? Intentional community.

Sure, all of us know about training partners like Arnold and Franco, who have always nodded to their training partnership as a secret to success.

But intentional communities (ICs) are bigger and deeper than training partners. First, they involve more people. Each of us brings something to the group, and honestly, the most important gift is showing up.

Second, an IC always welcomes more people to join in the fun.

Frankly, it's the new people who provide much of the direction. Most of us in our current group have been training over a decade. While that's great—congratulations and cigars all around—the downside of training so long is that we can easily forget the path.

When a new person joins our group, we ask, "What do you want to work on?" The answer can transform the next few weeks of training. Many people really want to learn and master the squat, but years of office work or poor training has made the basic movement either unwatchable or even dangerous.

So, we all step in with our gifts. Samantha Halpern is a physical therapist and might note that the person needs some of this corrective or that stretch. Marc, her husband and our go-to nutritionist, might add several points about the basics of good habits that extend well beyond the day's workout. Mike Brown might then take the person aside and find the right regression for the squat that clears things up, from rocking on the floor to holding on to the pole and squatting. And that's just a typical day.

This can be done between our lifting sets and general training. Often, most of us will also be doing the correctives and regressions the new person is doing because, well, it's a really good idea.

IC training also has another boon: I have a lot of experience in the weightroom, but sometimes I'm grouchy and tired. I need the youth and energy of the group to get my engine started. I like to offer them in return some positive feedback, some corrections and a general sense of "this is all okay."

My first IC started when I moved to California after half a lifetime in Utah. Dan Martin, an East Bay firefighter, asked if we could get together sometime to train. While the movers were unpacking boxes, I drove down to Coyote Point, and there we started a training group. Between piles of goose poop, we stretched, strained and trained. We only met once a week, but all of us looked forward to that weekly session.

When I returned to Utah, a group of young guys from the university asked if they could train with me two times a week. Soon it was three. Now, it's five.

When I visit my doctor, he asks if I train, and I answer, "At least an hour a day."

He remarks, "I have to admire your discipline."

I'm always honest with him: I only get out of bed because there will be people showing up at my door, ready to train.

Intentional communities also offer an additional advantage to those of us living (and often suffering) through the information age: We get a chance to hear summaries of blogs, books, articles and movies throughout the training session without having to invest the time in actually reading and watching all of them.

"Did you read that article on training adductors on website blah blah? What a waste."

Mental note—don't read it.

"This new book on habits and training is well worth a read." Borrow it.

"I can't believe how good this movie blah blah is. I was stunned."

Might be worth a view.

Since we're all internet savvy and interested in the best and brightest tools for fitness, health, longevity and performance, we share ideas across the whole swath of media, and then get back to the squat rack.

I've been lifting since 1965—yes, you read that right. That's a lot of six-week programs and crazy ideas and bad decisions. Of all the things I've done, *nothing* compares to the quality of having an IC.

Are there problems? Sure.

A common one is this: We have some people training, for example, for a kettlebell cert, while other are doing *Mass Made Simple*. I might be doing a twenty-one-day challenge of this kind or that. We have to ensure the equipment gets used in some kind of order. The upside is that most of us have squirreled away a few extra straps, bands, bells or wheels along the way, so we fix most problems by tossing more stuff into the mix.

Dan Martin calls this concept "Virtual Stone Soup." I realize now that most people today may not know this fine story anymore, so here it is—

> Some travelers come to a village, carrying nothing more than an empty pot. Upon their arrival, the villagers are unwilling to share any of their food with the hungry travelers. The travelers fill the pot with water, drop a large stone in it, and place it over a fire in the village square. One of the villagers becomes

curious and asks what they are doing. The travelers answer that they are making stone soup, which tastes wonderful, although it still needs a little bit of garnish to improve the flavor. The villager does not mind parting with just a little bit of carrot to help them out, so it gets added to the soup. Another villager walks by, inquiring about the pot, and the travelers again mention their stone soup, which has not reached its full potential yet. The villager hands them a little bit of seasoning to help them out. More and more villagers walk by, each adding another ingredient. Finally, a delicious and nourishing pot of soup is enjoyed by all.

Our communal training sessions are of this variety. We all bring tools from equipment to life experiences to sandwiches. We gather and train, work on issues and improve a little. We fall in love again with movement and muscle.

We reignite our passion for "all of this."

I have been training groups for so long that sometimes I ignore basic principles I learned the hard way. One of the keys to working in a group, especially in something physical, is to understand that you become part of an organism. The group becomes a living being.

That's why group training has such a big impact on long-term success: People do things they might not do otherwise, even with the best intentions. And we humans have this odd ability to handle more suffering if we do it as a group.

Moreover, it also seems more fun. I've had people vomit on my shoes and tell me thanks for the opportunity to do the work.

For the record, these are the best workouts of my life.

Your fitness goals—and those you help create for your clients—should expand life in all ways. Make the tiniest possible changes to health and longevity habits. Think "even smaller," like I did with the idea of a sip of water with each coffee or adult beverage.

Soon it will expand.

Next, find like-minded people and steal their energy—as they steal yours! Harness the power of the mind. You can use intense pain (painful words and physical pain both seem to work), slowly march ahead with small habits, follow the path of others, or use the power of community.

These all work. And, marvelously, they all work well together.

Chapter 8

Enough Is Enough and the Goldilocks Effect

Finding Just Right

Tiny habits and small changes underscore the key to applying the *Five Tools* appropriately to each and every client. Universally, we need to use the fifth tool—mental set—but *Threes*, for example, only need to add caloric restriction and inefficient exercise.

Don't do too much! Do what is needed, first and foremost. Be consistent. Enough is enough. Strive for "just right." That's the amount that can be done consistently, regularly and masterfully for long enough to insure progress.

I used to work with an oddball who spent most of his year drinking various green grass drinks, experimenting with living off of just sprouts and spending hours in various physical disciplines, with yoga being the tamest. When Lent came around, he would give up his health for the forty days. He smoked, drank coffee, ate bagels and basically acted like most people you know. He would get fatter, sicker and meaner and, honestly, I would begin to worry about him. His insight, though, was brilliant: He told me that by the time Easter Sunday came around, he loathed everything unhealthy and couldn't wait to eat and train with as much discipline as he could muster.

The lack of moderation in his lifestyle may not be for you or me. But I admire his insight: Having a little here or there just didn't work for him. He was either all in or he folded. The biggest issue most people have when it comes to training is that they have far too many options. We have a virtual buffet of equipment, exercise selections and programs. And these all work. They just don't all work at once.

If all you have to offer your clients is a barbell and a cellar, they can still make great progress. If you have a kettlebell and a backyard, they can make great progress. When you start adding too much stuff in terms of machines, equipment, magazines, heart rate monitors, books and all the rest, you start complicating something that should really be pretty simple.

As the late, great Charlie Francis said in his epic sprint workshop, the problem with most trainees is that "their *hards* are too easy and their *easys* are too hard."

In other words, most people train far too easy on their hard days, and then try to make up for it on their easy days by training too hard. It's such a simple point, but so many people miss it: *Most trainees rush to medium in all their training.*

Here's an illustration I often use. Your daughter comes home from college and tells you she found the man she wants to marry. She describes him as "medium height, medium build, so-so looks and an average student." How enthusiastic are you about your future son-in-law?

The same goes for medium training, in my humble opinion. I will do everything, including hiding all the tens, fives and various tiny plates, to make my clients commit to either training heavy or training light. This is what I call the "Goldilocks Effect."

As you hopefully remember, Goldilocks came upon the house of three bears. She discovered that porridge, chairs and beds seem to come in three basic styles that are perfect for thinking about weights: too heavy, too light and just right.

Keep "just right" floating around in your head for just a moment.

Now let's take a look at some equipment choices to understand the application of the Goldilocks Effect in a normal training session.

Eliminate the Excess

Early on with kettlebells, I found I could do basically every movement with each weight. If I wanted to snatch one hundred reps, the 16-kilo kettlebell would be easy, the 32-kilo kettlebell would be a challenge worthy of boasting, and the 24-kilo kettlebell would be just right.

When I work one-on-one with people, the number one thing I try to get them to do is eliminate the excess. If it's a home gym, I ask, "What do you use this piece of equipment for? Can you live without it?" I don't care what it's used for, but if a person can't tell me why that piece of equipment is in the gym, we get rid of it.

There's a documentary about computers that shaped the way I coach. At the time, it was thought that the world would probably only need five computers. This all changed one day when a programmer asked his friend about a new idea he was tossing around. "Does this have value?" he asked.

His friend, the head of an accounting firm, answered, "I hire four hundred people a week to do what you say I can do with the push of a button?"

"This" was the spreadsheet, and it changed the demand for computers. I began looking at equipment in a whole new light after seeing that documentary.

I watch idiotic YouTube videos where people use equipment to do all kinds of strange things. My favorite is a guy who tied himself to a tree to practice sprinting—the rope held him in place. One could also sprint without being tied to a tree, and I only mention this for clarity's sake.

People are fighting right now for our freedom to do any stupid thing we can think of, but let's honor them by doing the right moves with the right tools.

Barbells

I love barbells and have been using them since 1965. Here's why you need to have one: the press family and deadlifts. A typical barbell can be loaded with enough forty-five-pound plates to sneak up to seven hundred pounds. That is a lot of weight. You can also get the bar to jump from fifty-five pounds to sixty pounds if that's where your client is today. I've argued for years that if all we did was military or bench press and deadlift, we'd probably have most of our training locked in.

Moreover, competing in powerlifting (squat, bench press and deadlift) or Olympic lift (snatch, clean and jerk) makes a barbell a must.

TRX

My early knock on the TRX was that there was no solid information on how to use it. I questioned why I should have one. Here's why: The T, Y and I pulls, the single-arm rows and the double-arm rows target an area of the body that often gets missed or ignored. That whole area of the upper back and rear shoulders is probably the most underdeveloped area of people I work with. I've attempted odd variations of planks and dozens of pulls with other equipment, but the TRX answers these issues smarter and faster.

Kettlebells

I love the kettlebell (KB). Like my intern said the other day, it looks like you're training even while you're carrying them out to the car. Three moves make the KB irreplaceable: the goblet squat, the swing and the Turkish getup. Yes, you can use other things for these three moves, but the ease of transition and the feel of having the correct load in the right place—off-center in the Turkish getup and the swing—just makes a good KB worth having in your gym.

Mini-Bands

I never understood why anyone would use these until I was told to do one simple movement. The lateral walk with a mini-band around the socks (you really need to wear socks!) is the perfect way to light up and train the gluteus medius. A set of swings followed by a set of squats followed by a long lateral walk with mini-bands will teach your clients more about their butts than any anatomy class.

Ab Wheels

For ten dollars, you can do the best anterior chain ever invented, outside of a perfect pullup. I don't know of a workout, program or plan that couldn't be improved a bit by rolling out on one of these devices. You'll notice that these rise and fall in popularity, but here's my theory about why you don't see them much: Using them is really hard.

Dumbbells

You can do a lot of things with dumbbells, but we all know the knock on these in a gym. No matter how many are there in a rack, someone wants a weight that isn't there. I like dumbbells for farmer walks. All those really heavy dumbbells at the end of the rack that are covered in dust are perfect for using to walk around the gym while training literally every muscle in the body.

Combining these tools is the closest I've come to a perfect program, what I call the *Killer App* program—

- ♦ Barbell: Military or Bench Press

- ♦ TRX: T-Y-I Pulls and Rows

- ♦ Barbell or Kettlebell: Deadlift or Swings

- ♦ KB: Goblet Squat

- ♦ Dumbbells: Farmer Walk

- ♦ KB: Turkish Getup

- ♦ Ab Wheel: Ab Wheel Rollout

Get a limited amount of equipment and get back to simple and successful training. Pavel Tsatsouline has an interesting idea about lifting with barbells: only use forty-five-pound and twenty-five-pound plates. Toss the rest out! His idea is that to add load, a person would really need to have mastery of the weight before popping on another plate.

Working from Pavel's theory, we get this workout with the barbell—

- 95 pounds
- 135 pounds
- 145 pounds
- 185 pounds
- 195 pounds
- 225 pounds

To jump from 145 to 185 in some lifts is going to be a challenge. Your client will also fully appreciate the idea of "just right."

In the strength training universe, we have a problem that creeps up on those of us who use multiple pieces of equipment: How do I know which is hard, medium, easy or just right? When I write numbers like 225 or 405 in an article, column or book, how does the everyday person understand what these numbers mean?

I came up with an easy way to understand the number of repetitions—any motion or movement that's repeated and counted—and how that relates to load—the amount being moved, the weight or resistance.

Over the past sixty years, both experience and science has shown that between fifteen to twenty-five reps is about, around and close to the correct number of repetitions we need to do per exercise.

Here's how I judge—

- If it takes one or two sets to do the fifteen to twenty-five reps, the load is light.

- ♦ If it takes three, four, five or perhaps six sets to do the fifteen to twenty-five reps, the load is just right.

- ♦ If it takes more than seven sets, the load is too heavy.

Whether your client is using a machine, a band, a kettlebell, a dumbbell or whatever, this will help you determine when the load is just right.

There are days you'll want to go light, days you'll want to go medium, and days you'll want to challenge your clients with the heaviest load possible. Some experts argue that as few as a fifth of a person's workouts need to be challenging—and, of course, there are those who tell you that if you don't puke, you weren't trying.

I err on the side of more easy and medium workouts, as I keep thinking that showing up for five years without missing a training day will trump the person who has a surgery or illness every other month.

One of the people I read carefully in the strength field is Dave Tate. He once told me that when he sees a program that calls for 90 percent or above in the first few lines, he throws it away. He told our audience, "It might take some of us fifty-one weeks to build up to a 90 percent lift!" Clearly, when you have over a dozen guys bench-pressing 800 pounds, benching 720 every few days suddenly sounds heavy, doesn't it?

This works in the other direction, too. Clients who have never used weights before are going to be just as focused on wondering whether they're doing it right as they are on the load itself. We all needed to learn the fundamentals. It might take a hundred, a thousand or ten thousand repetitions of a movement before someone can honestly lean back and say, "This is right."

It's hard for most of us to understand the level of commitment it takes to achieve the highest levels of a sport. In the weightroom, we might need a decade to approach our best lifts. As I covered in my book, *Never Let Go*, we have four kinds of maximal performances—

1. *Sorta Max:* This is something I can do without any thought or effort. It's what most people think they can do.

2. *Max:* If someone special shows up while I'm training or I travel to another place and am spurred on by others or some charismatic coach, this would be my "best."

3. *Max Max:* This would be what I could do if I plotted and planned a performance for at least six months or maybe a year.

4. *Max Max Max:* This is that effort I guarantee has a story behind it. It's for a win, a championship or a lifesaving effort. Most people who hit this level probably doubt they can repeat it.

I'm not talking about just weights here either. How many hours of sleep do you need a night? Most of us will answer that we need at least eight hours in order to operate, but practically every parent has the story of a week or two of almost no sleep while caring for a sick child, and somehow continuing to put one foot in front of the other. I know someone who was in a seven-day battle in one of our wars, and nobody in his group took time off for a catnap.

But most of us at some level understand that a broad number like "percent of max" means very little in the reality of life. This is why I came up with the Goldilocks Effect.

For the majority of one's training career, we should use loads that are just right. For most of the classic workouts—five sets of three, three sets of five, five sets of five, and three sets of eight—you can see that the great tradition of strongmen, Olympic lifters and bodybuilders tends to emphasize the "just right" numbers.

Workouts with the Goldilocks Effect

Workouts, too, can benefit from this perspective. I've been preaching the idea of *Punch the Clock* workouts for almost a decade. *Punch the Clock* workouts are those sessions where we just show up and do the work. If there's a plan, follow it. If there's a preprinted workout, finish it. Much of training is this kind of thing, showing up and doing stuff—or SUDS: Show Up, Do Stuff.

It's also the kind of training that builds a system that will hold up over time. Still, there are times when the *Punch the Clock* workout should be left on the floor. The dog pukes in the car, the kids have a science fair and the roof leaks. Not every day is going to be a perfect day to follow a training plan.

Along with *Punch the Clock* workouts, I have workouts—short windows of training—I like to call challenges. I have all sorts of challenges, from the farmer walk challenge to my brother's 315 deadlift challenge. The farmer walk challenge is simply taking half of the trainee's bodyweight in each hand, where the total load is the person's bodyweight, walking as far as possible, and then coming back.

My brother offers a yearly challenge of doing as many reps with 315 pounds in the deadlift as one can in half an hour. For the record, my brother Gary is in his late sixties and is still doing this challenge.

But when these challenges turn into a program, I call them *Kill Yourself* workouts. Now, these can usually be survived for about three weeks. I remember back in junior high, our first football game was cancelled, so our coaching staff decided to sneak in an additional few more days of double sessions. We had three-and-a-half weeks of two training sessions a day, and our team dropped from seventy football players to about twenty-five. Our season was a disaster because we never really recovered from all the training.

Most gyms that push *Kill Yourself* workouts every session tend to have huge dropout rates and lots of physical therapy issues, and these gyms tend to close rather quickly. People certainly *can* do anything, but there's wisdom in *not* doing everything all the time.

My third kind of workout is the *Hangover Rule*. As I had conversations with people from all kinds of sports, I began noticing a pattern: Their lifetime best efforts were often the morning after a series of bad decisions at something like a bachelor party. Many of the stories included puking in flowerbeds, so perhaps that's the actual secret, but I think it's this: Expecting nothing, or very little, from a training session or competition often allows one to stretch and expand far beyond the usual constraints.

Do you have to be nursing a hangover for this to be true? No.

When I was eighteen, my coach, Dick Notmeyer, left on a road trip. I had to go into the city to train at the Sports Palace. My dad drove up with me (I needed him to pay the ten-dollar day fee), and soon I settled and started to train. My clean and jerks were feeling good that day, and when I walked through the door my personal best was 270. God bless kilos because I had to take 271, and clean and jerked it for a new PR.

My dad said it looked easy.

So I did 282.

Then I made 292.

Dan Curiel walked in and said, "Try 137.5 kilos. You can make it."

That's 303 pounds.

I made the lift and broke the three-hundred-pound barrier. I had added thirty-three pounds to my personal record in half an hour.

Why? I don't know and I don't ask. I've learned that extraordinary training sessions and days just pop out of nowhere, and you must enjoy your dance with these rare moments of life.

Certainly we should attempt to push forward and find our limits. But from my experience, regular training with appropriate loads brings our clients to their goals faster than trying to beat them into the ground day after day. Walking the path trumps crawling the path.

It also saves them from losing their minds.

Exercise Selection for Movement

Inefficient exercise (IE) is fun to think about—*What do I do really badly?*

That might be all that's needed.

For example, I've discovered that gymnastics work makes me sweat more than a sauna, so obviously something is going on in my cardiovascular system.

In the gym setting, kettlebell swings are the top of my list for IE. People will work very hard and go nowhere. Getting up and down off the ground is good, too, so mixing swings with pushups is a great way to get nowhere—save for fat loss—fast.

For hypertrophy and mobility training, I like to find movements that provide both at once. For example, the gymnastics dip and the one-arm bench press both demand a level of flexibility and mobility not found in the barbell bench press.

Consider—

♦ Push: Single-Arm Overhead Press, One-Arm Bench Press, Dip

- Pull: Single-Arm TRX Row and the variations of this movement

- Squat: Goblet Squat, Overhead Squat, Zercher Squat

- Hinge: Romanian Deadlift, Bulgarian Goat Bag Swing— all slow, nonballistic hinge movements

Find movements that stress a full range of motion and that can be done for reps in the eight to twelve range.

If someone needs basic strength training, I always think that something such as the *Killer App* program mentioned previously is a good starting point—

- Barbell: Military or Bench Press

- TRX: T-Y-I Pulls and Rows

- Barbell or Kettlebell: Deadlift or Swings

- KB: Goblet Squat

- Dumbbells: Farmer Walk

- KB: Turkish Getup

- Ab Wheel: Ab Wheel Rollout

Strength works better with fewer repetitions and more focus on load. When doing the key movements, do a total of ten reps after warmups.

Warmup
Five sets of the following

- Naked Turkish Getups, 5 per side

Can You Go?

- 15 Swings

- 1 Goblet Squat

- 10 March in Place

Press
Three sets of three

- 5 x 2, 2 x 5, 5-3-2 are all fine, too

Deadlift
Three sets of three

- 5 x 2, 2 x 5, 5-3-2 are all fine, too

TRX Rows
Three sets of fifteen

Finishers
One set of each

- Ab Wheel

- Lateral Mini-Band Walk

You can also take the concept of *Killer App* programming into the field of competition and stick to the same rules. My Olympic lifting coach, Dave Turner, had us train three days a week doing the following—

- Press: 5 x 3

- Snatch: 8 x 2

- Clean and Jerk: 8 x 1

- Front Squat: 5 x 2

- Farmer Walk

- Ab Wheel

To get strong, lift. It doesn't get any simpler than that.

If everyone was an eating, pooping, exercising machine, the first four tools would be all anyone would need. But, we're complex organisms with joys, sorrows, love, lust, highs and lows. So we need the fifth tool.

1. *Nutrition and caloric restriction*

2. *Inefficient exercise*

3. *Strength training*

4. *Hypertrophy and mobility training—the Fountain of Youth*

5. *Mental set*

For the self-coached, the poorly coached or those fortunate few with quality coaching, the fifth tool—the mental set—will be the key to long-term success. It's far better to be a good coach in this than in any other area, one who focuses on the dictum—

Train what is needed, not what is wanted.

Chapter 9

Coaching 101

What Is Good Coaching?

The fifth tool introduced the idea of coaching techniques. Good coaching involves an understanding of the goal-setting process and constant assessment. These two, goals and assessments, live in a feedback loop that keeps you and your clients on the right path.

Coaching tends to be as much an art as it is a science. I think of it as a chef adding carefully considered ingredients not found in the recipe in order to make something marvelous. Now, there's nothing wrong with following the recipe exactly from the cookbook of exercise programs, but you'll rarely find that what someone is doing in one part of the world is going to work in your local facility. It's nice to have the recipe, but you might not have the same ingredients.

Let's look at the art of coaching. Coaching really *is* like being a chef, but it's also the dance between goals and assessments. A coach has to be hands-on in the middle of all of it.

Percy Cerutty said—

> *The teachings of the coach must always be suspect when he attempts to develop techniques based upon theories worked out intellectually. Unless he gets the idea from personal experience and feelings first, he is most likely to be wrong in principle.*

We must be hands-on. We must assess as we address goals.

The 1-2-3-4 Assessment

This is where the *1-2-3-4 Assessment* comes in. It helps us in three distinct areas—

1. Clear out basic risks.
2. Highlight problems to address.
3. Outline a programming map.

As we're assessing, we're also listening to our clients' answers to our questions and hearing their general attitudes toward training, which leads to one final step.

Before I tell you what that step is, know that the bulk of the men we work with will be *Twos*. They need to do mobility work and they need some inefficient exercise.

But, they want to bench press. So, we have them to do a one-arm bench press—more of a mobility lift—mixed with something like swings or work on a rowing machine.

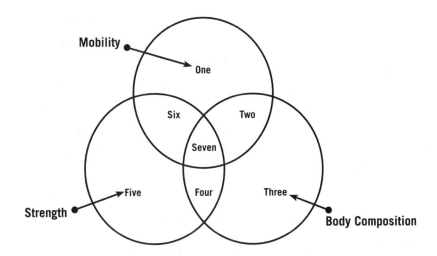

Most women will be *Fours*. They need to be barbell squatting, benching and deadlifting.

With experience, you'll discover, too, that what people *need* to do is rarely what they want to do.

As you assess, you'll need to get inside the head of your client. This step is judgmental. Now, many of my college students tell me, "I don't like to judge." Well, if you want to be a teacher, coach, trainer or leader, you'd be wise to learn to judge!

In the business of working with people's bodies, your judgment not only helps them along the path to their goals, but it is often the key to safety.

Relaying this next assessment to your client is going to require some *savoir faire*, the ability to quickly adapt in any situation.

Good coaching is good teaching. The following are the three qualities of a good teacher—

1. *The Know:* mastering the vast body of information regarding the subject matter—and that can still take years after achieving an advanced degree

2. *The Do:* having a number of ways to teach and deliver the information—traditionally, this is fourfold: tell a story, show a picture, ask questions and memorize blocks of information, of which songs and poetry are the best examples

3. *The Savoir Faire:* being able to swiftly adapt to anything in order to convey information in a way that feels innate

I don't share the following with clients, but I've found that stopping for just a moment and categorizing their relationships to training is helpful in determining where to go from square one.

Basically, I place clients into one of five categories as I discern their relationships to training—

1. Untrained
2. Detrained
3. Overconditioned and undertrained
4. Dazed and confused
5. Well trained—those seeking mastery

Untrained

This is often the best category to work with, as untrained people generally don't carry a lot of baggage from poor training programs, overtraining issues and additional information they may not need. With untrained people, corrective work usually means teaching the techniques of training and doing the fundamental human movements since they don't have a lot of injuries to contend with.

Detrained

Most trainers and coaches will agree that these people are often the worst. The more "I used to…" stories you hear, the harder the road ahead. If the person has tried thirty diets, any nutritional advice you give is attempt number thirty-one. Get ready for "I used to do this," "my coach used to have me do that," and all kinds of stories of former glory. You might need to regress most movements to fewer ballistic moves, and demand adherence to beautiful technique.

Overconditioned and Undertrained

Overconditioned and undertrained—these are people who have learned ten thousand different ways to do the most elaborate and difficult moves in every sport or gym movement, but can't seem to do five pushups. They tend to raise their hands all the time at workshops to discuss the trivia of training, but can't do the first minute of the warmup. If you have any experience training or coaching, you've worked with people from this category. These people are very hardworking, who will always demand to be puking and sweating to call a workout "good." Often, though, their technique and mastery of fundamental human movements are hurtful to watch. It will take a lot of convincing to change their minds that, long-term, there's a better way to do it.

Dazed and Confused

This group includes the great mass of people who are convinced that fruit makes them fat…or is it coffee? Lifting makes them weak and stiff, but running is good and bad. Whenever I read a fitness magazine, I feel this way, too. Good quality information about diet and fitness never makes the headlines. To help our *Dazed and Confused* friends, talk about what Grandma cooked, and how people stayed in shape before the advent of the information age. Walking the dog and eating home-cooked food is not a bad start.

Well Trained

These are people who seek mastery, who appreciate the highs and lows of daily, weekly, monthly and decadely training, and who seek something always larger, even if it's tough to define. Yes, I wish this were everyone who walks into the gym. Our task is to get people on the road to mastery, no matter where they're coming from.

The Road to Mastery

I want my clients to be on the road to mastery.

When discussing mastery I'm always reminded of Roger Bannister and David Hemery. Both were noted British athletes, Bannister famously breaking the four-minute mile, and Hemery winning the 1968 Olympics in the four-hundred-meter hurdles. Both were famous for using pen and paper to prioritize training into achievable, doable, smaller goals. Hemery, by the way, continued on this path well beyond his Olympic years by competing in the original *Superstars* television contests. He addressed extra training such as gymnastics and canoeing so he could dominate the events for years.

As coaches we have to be adaptable to deal with this variety of visions about training. Putting a program and system in place requires *savoir faire.* It also requires adherence to basic principles.

I know you're going to have some *Sevens* argue that they need a much more advanced program because back in the day they could jump over buildings and survive on cat food for months at a time. This is why I think it helps to prepare before discussing this by learning how to talk with a deconditioned client as opposed to an overconditioned or an undertrained client.

And, truly, this is *Intervention*, the skill to sit with clients and calmly explain what's going on in their training. This is why we do the full *1-2-3-4 Assessment*; you need a fair amount of evidence to get people to try this other path toward their goals.

Still, no matter what sound advice we share, we'll always face the problem of the prettier, curvier, sexier program that's always right around the corner. You need to wrap your arms around this idea: *A reasonable approach will always be challenged by the excitement and enthusiasm of the next big thing.*

Reasonable training isn't nearly as exciting as the next big thing, or as I like to call it, the BBD. Whenever I read an article on the internet about fitness, I always shudder when I read the comments. No matter what the topic, no matter what the point, if there's a feedback or comment box after the article, someone is going to post a BBD.

BBD stands for "Bigger, Better Deal."

When I discussed a yearlong approach to losing a single pound in a year—better than what 99 percent of us will do this year—a post appeared: "I lost sixteen pounds in three weeks doing the RX45!"

Often, the people posting are directing you to their affiliate site so they can make a little extra cash, but I digress. Absolutely, no question about it, no matter what you do, no matter how well you do it, someone is going to tell you there's a better way!

We see BBDs everywhere. Throw a world record, and someone will give you an idea about how to toss farther. I am sure somebody told Wilt Chamberlain that if he'd have shot better than thirty-six for sixty-three, he would have easily scored more than the one hundred points that night in 1962.

A lot of BBDs are caused by the overwhelming amount of information available today. I just checked Amazon.com and discovered if you read two books a week on diet, not including cookbooks, it would take you sixty-five years to finish all that magic bookseller carries. I will die happy not doing that.

If we put together every training method, some will argue one set of exercise versus multiple sets of exercise. Some methods ask for whole-body days, and others split the body into parts. Some argue that we should train the lungs and the body will follow, or that we should train the legs and the lungs will just have to keep up.

No matter what, if you follow the next three points, you'll be fine as a trainer or a coach. None of them is new or original (the first goes back to Hippocrates), but adherence to these three ideas will keep you happy and sane throughout your career—

1. Do no harm.
2. Keep the goal the goal.
3. Almost universally, someone has done it before you. Follow them!

Personally, I follow what the best and brightest do to achieve any goal. I ask physique models about fat loss, and powerlifters about increasing strength.

Do what the clients need before you do what they want.

Have them follow an appropriate training program and way of eating.

Ensure they finish the program.

Finally, constantly assess: Keep an eye on the goal and be comfortable with minor changes to pursue it.

Once you've assessed, what comes next is simple—

1. Do what is needed.
2. Design an appropriate program.

3. Finish the program!

4. Reassess.

Troubleshooting: An Attempt to Deal with Obstacles

Troubleshooting is a wonderful word. It's a great way to describe the value of exercise correction. When a client is doing a move and there seems to be an issue, some trouble, your task is clear: Look to find the source of this trouble and address it.

Sadly, all too often we see trainers doing too much or not enough.

I can only imagine what's going on in the inner dialogue.

"I'm getting paid to do something."

"Hmmm…what can I do? I have it: I will count reps."

Folks, if you merely count reps, please hire a kindergarten student to do this instead, as this practice will really help the five-year-old learn to count. Getting paid to count reps is embarrassing, to say the least.

Then the next point goes flashing through our trainer's mind.

"Maybe I can correct this movement. That's it exactly: I will point out an issue."

This is what I call looking for trouble.

Let me address two issues first. Number one, in God's infinite wisdom, God decided not to make us all the same. If you ever see a professional basketball player standing next to a female Olympic gymnast, you'll immediately see that legs come in all different lengths.

Teaching someone really tall to squat is a quick lesson in measurements: The bar is going to move several feet. Teaching a perfectly built person who was born to squat involves watching the bar moving as little as a few inches.

Yet some of us strive to teach a single style—in other words, everyone should look the same.

Stu McGill really opened my eyes about this with his explanation of the hips. Some of us are built to toss cabers, and some of us were born to squat heavy and deep. And over there, that guy was born to sprint faster than me. Oh, I can push a car up a hill faster than he ever will, but he'll beat me in a short race each and every time.

Second, we humans have our eyes facing forward. Under load, it's hard to see what someone means when they say you have a "butt wink" or "knee collapse."

In fact, words often fail an athlete under load or stress.

As an outside observer, the trainer and coach are seeing things. The person performing the movement is performing.

Correcting a person's movement is a bit of a conundrum: Too much correction leads to no movement, and too little leads to flailing, ugly efforts.

Certainly we need to troubleshoot. Just don't try to make trouble by looking for it. A better way to think of this is as managing risks.

Managing Risks: Protecting the System

Much of the *1-2-3-4 Assessment* is simply managing risks. When we ask a client to stand on one foot, measure the height and waist, and to get up and down off the floor, we're addressing the simplest tests of a safe life.

A life blessed with both longevity and good health demands a little risk management.

My daughter, Lindsay, is in a sorority. Neither my wife nor I did the Greek life, so this was new territory for us. As her dad, I have been very pleased with this decision. There's a skill set acquired when you live with forty to eighty people in a small area.

In addition, part of the mission of every fraternity and sorority is to instill the qualities of leadership.

Lindsay, like all her sorority sisters, was given lessons on leadership. It was an attempt to distill the experiences of women who had walked those halls before and had learned some hard-earned lessons.

Lindsay explained to me an issue with managing risks. It was a discussion about social gatherings involving alcohol. There were rules that seemed obvious, simple and logical, like not serving underaged drinkers and ensuring food was available. Nonmember hosts and bartenders were insisted upon. The one rule that caught my eye was that these nonmember bartenders had to agree, in writing, not to be armed.

I don't know what happens at sorority parties, but if the bartenders have to agree not to carry firearms…I might not want to know more.

These are the basics of risk management. There are things we do in life that are risky. Frankly, life is risky. Surviving birth, early childhood diseases, traffic, sports and those moments you announce "hold my beer and watch this" have always seemed to be miraculous to me.

Longevity still comes down to the basics.

Years ago, Dick Notmeyer told me that long life comes down to roughly the following formula—

- Genetics: 50 percent

- Habits: 40 percent

- Luck: 10 percent

There are some people born lucky when it comes to longevity. We often read of families with siblings all in their nineties. Now, *quality* of life is a whole other topic, but it seems some people live longer no matter how hard they try to sabotage nature. Somebody always has a story about a whiskey-drinking, cigarette-smoking uncle who lived to 120. That's like telling me your cousin is seven feet tall—sometimes, you just have the genes for it.

I insist upon good habits, but let's not overlook luck. As an example, I was born just after the great advances in penicillin. I also contracted several lung diseases as an infant, and my baby book is filled with doctor's visits and injections. Literally, I was lucky to be born after these advances.

As another example, I have a good friend who tells the story of how he was about to go over to a tent to grab something, when his buddy told him he would go. A Japanese mortar shell hit the tent, and his buddy died instantly. The story still haunts my friend seventy years later.

Perhaps luck doesn't explain it well enough, but most people understand the point. You can be in the wrong place at the wrong time. It happens, and a slip here or a collision there can alter or end your life.

In the *1-2-3-4 Assessment*, we discuss a few ways to increase luck that don't make the Venn diagram:

1. Keep bodyweight under three hundred pounds.

2. Exercise about a half hour every day.

3. Eat colorful vegetables.

And that's it. I'm sure my mother could have told us all of this without the lab coats and the research money.

So, managing risk for most of us is going to be pretty simple: Do the daily basic safety tasks of life, eat your veggies and go for a walk.

Sadly, most people ignore the simple stuff and want to know about some cutting-edge supplement that can only be found in a remote wilderness and that costs a month's salary. No daily walk, no supplements.

Yet this is precisely the problem with most people. They want the exotic answer—the trick, the secret, the inside information, the scoop, the skinny, the real story—when the truth is this: Go for a walk and eat a colorful salad.

There are two sides to managing risks for health, fitness and performance.

+ First, minimize risks by following the basics of safety.

+ Second, strive to do the minimal minimum—the same daily exercise and same basic dietary standards.

In a nutshell, the goal of any program is to increase "ready."

My career path involved eight or nine years of general and specific training, and then I was ready to throw far.

When your moment comes on the big stage of life, you're ready. The lead actor of a Broadway play gets ill, and you become the toast of New York. You step up to the plate when the starter goes down, and swing yourself into the Hall of Fame.

You make the lift, close the deal, raise the roof and ring the bell.

Bend, Don't Break

We as trainers and coaches need to get our clients to the point where they "bend, but don't break." They need to build up a little resilience in their lives, a bit of wiggle room, a bit of flexibility.

I'm reminded of one of the basics of personal finance: having an emergency fund. Things come up. A high school kid probably could get away with a hundred dollars in an envelope for some fine or expense that might pop up, rather than involving Mom and Dad.

For most of life, somewhere around one or two thousand dollars might be enough. This is enough, from my experience, to pay for a new water heater on Christmas Eve.

If you have the money close at hand, sure, you might bend a bit as you lose it, but you won't break.

Sometimes, a friend, a teammate or a community can stand in for you, but we want you to consider the next step: Be ready when it's your turn.

Stay on the Right Path: Three Principles of Coaching

I follow three basic coaching principles to insist that I stay on the right path. The three are interlocking and perhaps obvious to some. They are—

+ The prisoner's dilemma

+ Little and often over the long haul

+ Concept–Drill–Frankenstein's monster

First, I have often challenged coaches and trainers with *the prisoner's dilemma,* and now I'm going to pose it to you: If, for whatever reason, you were only allowed three fifteen-minute sessions a week, what would you do?

Now, don't worry about why you're only allowed three short sessions—imagine you're a political prisoner or something. To reach your goals, what would you do?

However you answered that question should be the core of your training. As a discus thrower, I would do full turns into a wall with a powerball, and snatch and squat after every ten throws.

Josh Hillis's answer for fat loss was brilliant: "I'd do food preparation!"

What this question asks and answers is what you consider the core, the fundamentals, of the path to the goal.

The answer can often be stunning. One baseball coach told me he wouldn't do much batting as that's a skill that doesn't necessarily improve with practice.

Ask the question, and make the answer be the core of your future programming.

Now take this a step forward. Once a client has identified this, your job as coach is to insist that the person actually does it!

Item two, *little and often over the long haul,* is a phrase I first heard from Coach Ralph Maughan, but many have used the concept. If you want to be good in the discus, lift weights three days a week and throw the discus four days a week for the next eight years.

Most people miss that last part—for the next eight years.

If your client wants to be great in the discus, I don't have a two-week program for you. The thrower is going to have to go out to that prison courtyard and toss and lift for a long time.

There are no overnight sensations in mastery. We have to be in it for the long haul.

The *Concept–Drill–Frankenstein's monster* approach keeps us from mastering in minors. When I teach a movement, I begin with the big picture, the concept. If a client understands the concept, I don't worry about drilling or breaking it down further. This person is good to go.

For example, the concept for squatting is to squat *between* the legs, not *on* the legs. If your athlete naturally drops between the thighs, you might be good to go. Congrats.

Drills are valuable in schooling the concept if something is missing or something needs more work. Sometimes, yes, the drill is the skill, but don't ever let drilling get in the way of the big picture of things.

But of the three, it's the Frankenstein part that gets most of us in trouble. Frankenstein's monster was a collection of parts, and some people think this is the way to coach.

"This is your ankle."

"This is your knee."

Ignore the individual parts as long as you can. Let the body and mind figure it out. Only after a lot of reps that are still subpar should you look for the limiting joint or muscle.

I recommend combining these three principles as often as you can. Decide on the key to the goal—*what's the core.* Then schedule plenty of weeks or months to address it. And when it's time to correct something, step back to see the whole picture. Take your time with sub-movements, the drilling, and, finally, look at the smaller units.

Now that we know what your client's goals are and where the person is in life, it's time to determine the development of the qualities needed to get to point B. At the end of the day, we need to assess everybody, and as we say in our gym, if you ain't assessing, you're guessing.

Chapter 10

The Coach's Ten Commandments for Keeping the Goal the Goal

Stay on Track!

No matter what your clients look like and no matter what their goals, the *Coach's Ten Commandments for Keeping the Goal the Goal* will help keep you and your clients on track.

These ten principles are important to coaching in the best way for each and every client.

1. *Train appropriately for the goal.*

2. *Train little and often over the long haul.*

3. *The longer it takes to get in shape, the longer the shape will remain.*

4. *Warmups and cooldowns really do play important roles.*

5. *Train for volume before intensity.*

6. *Cycle the workouts.*

7. *Train in a community.*

8. *Train the mind.*

9. *Keep the training program in perspective.*

10. *Fundamentals trump everything else.*

1. Train appropriately for the goal.

The best advice I can give here is to find someone who has already achieved your client's goal. This can be that simple, but you have to be careful. When I was coming up as a discus thrower, I was lucky to have all kinds of people to talk to about training, people who were better discus throwers than me. Some of the advice was wrong, but most of it was right.

Wrong advice in some things might be deadly. Use common sense as often as you can.

Again, I was lucky and had some good advice that kept turning up over and over.

It was clear I had to learn the Olympic lifts, so I did. I had to throw a lot, so I did. For your clients, call someone who has achieved the goals and apply their good advice. It's a rare day that I don't talk with some amazing people from all kinds of backgrounds who can point me in the right direction.

The reason I talk about fat loss a lot, besides the fact that it's a popular topic, is that many of my friends are in the business of training people in fat loss. I hear stuff all the time and, in total candor, sometimes it's stupid. But usually it circles around to things that work.

Find someone who has been there. Find someone who has walked the walk. And train appropriately.

2. Train little and often over the long haul.

It's difficult to envision achieving a goal four to eight years in the future. I think part of great coaching is the ability to whittle the dozens of tasks and details into small chunks, and still keep an eye on the whole project.

Coach Maughan told me about "little and often over the long haul" back in 1977 when he discussed his approach to making a great thrower. He believed a thrower—

- Should lift with the basic movements three days a week

- Should take time off after the season to regroup and refresh

- Should throw three to five times a week after the refresher period

- Should do this for seven or eight years before deciding to add more work

Of course, I disagreed with all of this! He had merely coached a couple of great throwers and a world-record holder, but I was twenty-one. What did he know? Of course, he was right. And, at age twenty-one, I was wrong about a lot of things.

Coach Maughan believed in attaining mastery without a lot of injuries, and in growing up in all areas of life. If you go to college for five years, for example, and compete at a high level but don't get your degree, you have missed mastery across the rest of your life.

That's why I always laugh when someone wants to be great at an Olympic sport well after a certain age. Someone once asked if I could do just one thing to improve my O lifting, what would it be?

"Start at age eight."

I was partially joking, but it's the truth. Excellence takes time in hours over time in years.

3. The longer it takes to get in shape, the longer the shape will remain.

My knock on quick-fix programs has always been the Day 91 issue. You do a program for ninety days…great, but then what? I tell my fat-loss clients, "If it took twelve years to put it on, at least give me a few weeks to help get it off."

The same holds true for getting in shape. A six-week off-season training program might do wonders—and it can—but if a client's season lasts half a year, we're going to be scrambling to keep all of the qualities needed to compete. This concept lives in a symbiotic relationship with the second commandment of "little and often over the long haul."

The longer a client takes to get in shape or to prep for an event, the longer the qualities seem to stay around. That's just one of my knocks on the use of performance-enhancing drugs: I've seen guys change overnight, but on the other hand, the losses are overnight, too. Strength seems to stay for a long time if it's built up over a long time.

This is the secret to what I was told by one of my heroes, Glenn Passey. Passey weighed 178 pounds when he won the national championship and broke Utah State's school discus record. When I finally got the chance to meet him, he told me that he "didn't lift weights like you guys do now." He explained that he lifted weights maybe five months a year with just the Olympic lifts. Then he'd stop. The next year, he'd pick up weights again, get back to the previous year's lifts within a few workouts, and see some nice progress.

This approach would continue over his college and post-collegiate experience. Passey's approach was a decade-long vision of preparing an athlete to get strong as easily as possible, and holding on to those strength levels over time.

For both a yearly approach and one that reaches across an athlete's career, the longer we spend getting into condition, the longer those gains seem to hold. It's so logical and reasonable, it's a wonder why people break this simple recommendation so often.

4. Warmups and cooldowns really do play important roles.

I try to make my warmups and cooldowns seamless, literally so built-in that clients might not know we've changed gears. But there's a need for both of these key elements.

I like to think of a warmup in waves: You first let the little ones splash over you, then you take your time getting out into the bigger waves.

The answer to how long and how much of a warmup is needed is going to depend on a lot of factors. Sometimes, none is needed!

I learned this lesson in my sophomore year in college when we arrived at a track meet and heard the announcement, "Last call, men's discus."

That couldn't be right!

It turned out we had the wrong schedule—and it was right. I went down to the track, dressed behind a very supportive group of new friends, stepped into the ring for my first throw, with no warmup, and threw really well. My second throw was my lifetime best.

Sometimes, the whole workout can be "only" a warmup. I recommend this for everyone about twice a month just to get the body feeling in tune again. And it's always a good idea to do this the day before a competition.

For the rest of the time, I like to think more like a jazz musician, where we play around with movements, intensities, reps and volume to get the body ready for the work at hand. Playfulness is valuable in the warmup, and perhaps even more importantly, in the cooldowns as it helps keep clients coming back.

And, if there's a secret to all this, it's to keep coming back.

5. Train for volume before intensity.

Barry Ross took Pavel's *Power to the People* template of dead-lifts and presses, and applied it to the world of sprinting. When you first read his programming ideas, the lack of volume on the track and in the weightroom is shocking. But it's only shocking because you haven't read the rest of his work!

If someone suddenly makes unbelievable progress switching from a volume program to an intensity program, you shouldn't be surprised. This is common, and it's the approach track coaches have used for at least a century. The pyramid model of training might have flaws, but it's hard to argue that we need to build a peak by ensuring a broad base. Getting in the volume helps build that base.

Once the base is there, it tends to last—see number three above. But at some point we also have to have the courage to walk away from volume so we can up the intensity. Not everyone likes to do this, as there's some joy and comfort in those "medium" workouts that feel good. Intensity can make a person nauseous.

Ross has a marvelous conditioning program made up of twelve fifteen-minute walks with one rule: Go farther each time, but never jog or run. People fall in love with Ross's deadlift and sprint workouts, but they tend to miss this little gem of conditioning.

6. Cycle the workouts.

I'm always dismayed when people show me these twenty-six–week workouts they're about to begin. In twenty-six weeks, something is going to come up to interfere with their plans.

Instead, I love two-week blocks and constant vigilance concerning omissions, errors, poor movement and lack of mobility.

The reason I like two-week blocks is that most people—even the worst of us who can't follow a plan for more than a minute without trying to make it better—can survive two weeks without too many life changes.

Not long ago, I was challenged by a "fitness expert" who disagreed with me. This high school junior had a program that had bodybuilding, Olympic lifting, powerlifting, plyometrics and all the rest in one complete program. The issue with this kid, God love him, was that he had cobbled together several high-end, elite programs, and had decided to go all-in and take care of everything at once.

Everyone knows it isn't going to work, because adaption is the king of performance, and doing everything won't lead to adaption everywhere. I do wish it could work, though!

7. Train in a community.

First, success leaves tracks. Constantly follow the successful tracks of others, but don't forget, second, that community increases intensity. As I mentioned earlier, I've been involved with several clubs of people who get together to train. All of them helped me train better and smarter. By myself, I might not do "one more round" of follow-the-leader presses, but with other people around, it's easy to press on.

With these experiences, I've expanded my understanding of correctives and my ability to teach using heart rate monitors. In my experience, the teacher in these groups learns the most.

8. Train the mind.

Tommy Kono says the mind is fifty percent of the performance. I'm not going to disagree.

Yogi Berra told us that "90 percent of it is half mental."

I'm not sure what you're doing, but there's a mental training tool, technique or tip that's going to help you. I've used affirmations, guided meditations, right- and left-brain work, goal-setting work and other methods to "get my head right."

This is the ticket to success in any goal-setting experience. Success leads to more success in so many ways. I've told every one of my state champions that "one day, the lessons you learned here are going to carry over to success in every area of your life."

Most agree within a year that successfully plotting a championship course requires the same set of tools as graduating from college or putting a career together. The right mental tools—the right mental toughness—carries over into all aspects of life.

9. Keep the training program in perspective.

It's just a gold medal or world record. In the big picture of things, not everything we do is epically important. I'll keep this one short: There are more important things in life than six-pack abs.

10. Fundamentals trump everything else.

Yes, it's going to be the fundamentals—the basics—that bring everything home: fundamental movements, basic flexibility and mobility, basic techniques and basic nutrition.

Chapter 11

The Big Picture of Training Systems

Setting the Stage

Assessment and goal setting set the stage for discovering what is needed. Utilizing the *Five Tools* appropriately gets us on the path toward this goal, this need. Proper basic coaching tools ensure we don't stray too far from the path. With enough experience, practice and community, we can soon channel each client into a system that supports their goals and continuing assessment.

Athletes, as I often tell the general population, make a deal with the devil. To be a great thrower, you have to be asymmetrical. Socrates told discus throwers to throw with both hands to remain balanced, and this is excellent advice even today, but the competition calls for a single good throw with one arm. Collision athletes will suffer with all kinds of trauma for the rest of their lives, and endurance athletes face a cascade of issues from joint stress to organ problems.

T. H. White once said, "The most difficult thing in the world is to know how to do a thing and to watch someone else do it wrong without comment."

As a strength coach, personal coach or personal trainer, there's no need to make things worse rather than better. The way to ensure you're seeking better is to examine your systems for training.

I like to spend my coaching time working on movement. Whether it's the turn in the discus or the pull of the Olympic lifts, I find that hands-on movement coaching is the most satisfying.

And, like White notes, keeping my mouth shut and allowing the process of learning to happen is the hardest part. It's going to take a lot of repetitions and time, and oftentimes the biggest obstacle to mastery is my big mouth.

When you do step in to coach, be sure that your instruction is clear, concise and correct.

Rarely do people ask questions about proper, repeatable quality movement. Most of the questions I answer deal with programs, programming, peaking and planning. The follow-up question I almost universally ask, besides "What's your goal?," is "What's your system?"

A system is not a collection of parts. I know I overuse the idea of Frankenstein's monster, but a good system isn't just a collection of pieces sewn together, then sparked with lightning. A system can be built upon, simplified, transferred and passed down. A system is certainly full of parts, but the parts work together as a whole, and a good system is recognized when the whole is greater than the sum of the parts.

I want you to understand what a fitness or performance system should be by using these three rules—

1. Addition by subtraction.

2. Additional components must improve the overall organism.

3. The system survives the loss of its founder.

First, I want you to step back and look at your program—your system—from another perspective. I argue that the best thing to do is to ask your clients. "What are we doing? What's working? What's making us successful?"

The key is this: You need to listen closely to the answers. There's a chance your clients have no idea what your training plan is!

For the self-coached, ask yourself—or someone who has been training with you—*what seems to work for me?*

I have a note in my 1992 journal that says, "I seem to make my best progress training hard three days a week and very easy the rest of the time."

When I shared this with Tiffini, she said, "Of course you do. I know that."

It had taken me over twenty-five years to come to that insight.

What we need to understand before we move on to five sets of five on the bench press or twenty minutes of stationary bicycling is the *system* you're trying to install with your group.

People think I'm joking when they ask me how I train track athletes, but it all comes down to this—

+ Throwers throw.

+ Jumpers jump.

+ Sprinters sprint.

+ Runners run.

+ Hurdlers hurdle.

For a high school hurdler to hit his stride in competition with ten hurdles in the way and people flailing right and left, he needs around fourteen competitions. Some states put strict restrictions on total meets, but it takes that many to get used to the noise and confusion of competing. Most hurdlers train with just three hurdles, over and over, and it's not a surprise that many kids hit hurdles four and five. They've literally never seen hurdles four and five before, and certainly never with other people at their elbows.

There's more to success than just recruiting, coaching and competing. We also have to model some very important keys that will keep people coming back to us.

It's Our Fault

If Thom Plummer is right, and I think he is, 86 percent of the American population doesn't belong to, attend or join gyms, community centers or fitness clubs. After high school, most people opt out of organized fitness. True, we might buy suspect items hawked on late-night TV, but it's a rare person who joins a gym.

Even rarer is the person who *goes* to the gym.

And it's our fault.

Many people seem to enjoy belittling the efforts of our friends and neighbors. We've all seen it. This belittling leads me to a rant: I don't approve of Fat Man's Relays at high school track meets. This is the event where the throwers go out and do a relay race. First, seriously, in this day and age, we're calling our male and female athletes "fat," and then getting a chuckle out of their flailing efforts to sprint around a track.

Great idea.

This is one of my key pillars to long-term success as a coach, and I quote, *"Don't make me look stupid!"*

I love elegance, mastery and grace above all in sports and life, and making fun of someone for not having had the time, opportunity or genetics to succeed is against everything I ever learned from the quality people in my life.

How can we live in community, both in sports and in the world, where the highlight of the day is to ignore elegance, mastery and grace, and to laugh at the poor efforts of others?

This is the big picture to me. Can we actively achieve our goals and maintain the life balance?

I have a simple five-part formula that knits together the focused needs of goal setting with the reality of living as a human in community. In the center of the vision are goal setting and ongoing assessment. The goal-setting part of the formula, for me, as a strength coach and friend, is when I simply ask clients, "What's your goal?"

Getting to a goal requires ongoing assessment, and whether it's using the Functional Movement Screen, strength tests, blood tests, body-comp tests, flexibility tests or timed drills, assessments give us an idea of where we are today.

The first day I did the Olympic lifts, Dick Notmeyer told me that the bare minimum for a lifter was a bodyweight snatch. At my first meet three weeks later, I did that, and then Jim Schmitz told me that very soon I would snatch what I clean and jerked (231) that day. And I did that in nine months.

That little history lesson reminds us that clear standards are an efficient tool for guiding people from here to there.

I'm a big fan of resolutions and goal setting, as I'm sure you know by now. One of the keys to my success as a coach, I believe, has been my ability to see that ongoing adherence to goal setting needs three additional points—

♦ Results!

- ◆ Don't make me look stupid!

- ◆ Community involvement

Results!

When I talk about results at a workshop, I have to hold back the urge to say, "obviously." Yet results are often overlooked in fitness and health discussions. Spend five minutes on the various chest-pumping sites on the internet—there have been wars with less macho posturing than some people's discussions about their combinations of squats and pushups.

We see numbers, times, unwatchable videos and all kinds of avatars with various warriors from *300* or some other blood-lust film. Yet when I go to a gathering and meet these same internet warriors, it's often hard to tell if any of them lift weights—or even train in some manner at all.

Training comes down to results. It's so obvious that it's hard to type it.

That's why I love the sports that have made my career, throwing and lifting. If we add this or that to our training and I throw farther or lift more, whatever we did was right—which we know because we saw the *results*.

So, here again is what you need to first ask your clients: *What is your goal?*

For body-comp goals, where are the before-and-after pictures, the measurements and the fat-loss measurements?

Don't guess, do. That's the key here.

Think of it this way: If you want to be a Navy SEAL, have you joined the Navy? If you want to be in the NFL, are you playing for a team now?

It's that clear in my head.

Beyond that, is the training producing results?

If you're making a living in fitness, your clients are your best advertising. That's why before-and-after pictures are so important for selling your skills. John Berardi, Josh Hillis and many others have made the use of these pictures mainstream, but it's really a simple idea—here's where I am, and this is where I was.

If we're making progress, things are working.

I use results to test programs and programming. After a review of my journal, which I've kept since 1971, I realized that the two best programs I ever did for pure strength and preparedness for throwing consisted of only two workouts a week. Pavel came to the same insight with this program—

Day One

+ Bench Press

+ Squat

Day Two

- ◆ Bench Press

- ◆ Deadlift

I switched the deadlift with cleans or snatches, and made the best progress of my life. Of course, as we all know, it worked so well, I stopped doing it.

Don't Make Me Look Stupid

The next key to ongoing progress is something I missed for a long time: *Don't make me look stupid.*

Putting a fourteen-year-old girl in the varsity football weight-lifting class is going to make her look stupid. As hard as she tries, she'll always stand out in the class because of her gender and the obvious need to lighten the load.

Making an overweight mother of three do something that she fails at in public usually isn't going to keep her coming back for more.

This is why I constantly discuss the need for mastery of movements and a certain amount of grace in training.

You know it when you see it, like a great baseball player moving toward a ball. I suggest reading the fiction work *The Art of Fielding* by Chad Harbach for some really interesting insights on this topic.

When I coach mastery of movement, I actively work against the issue of *Don't make me look stupid.*

It doesn't mean I don't challenge the athlete, the middle-age woman or the fourteen-year-old girl. Certainly I do. But with proper coaching cues, enough repetitions and appropriate regressions and progressions of movement, everyone can look masterful while training. Ignoring this, in my experience, kills progress, and the person quits and moves on to something else.

Appropriate Community

The third quality that supports goal achievement is appropriate community. Whenever I advise a new gym owner, I talk about safety, cleanliness and a vision of training that will keep people coming back. Then I talk about community outreach, from canned food drives to pushups for charity and anything else that will get the name of the gym out to the public in a positive way.

But there's also the need for internal community.

One of my best memories of coaching is taking two hurdlers and fourteen throwers to a track meet. I had just finished reading a book that emphasized that rich people cheer the success of other rich people. It struck me that this was a tool we used with our teams at Skyline College and Utah State.

"Team" is the key here, and many may have forgotten that some of us were trained to put country, church, team and family ahead of our own needs and desires. Don't worry, I fail miserably on this teaching just about every time my brain sparks a synapse.

With that track group that day, my idea was to encourage the kids to madly cheer for each other to set personal records. It was magic. Not only did we take the first six places in the girls' discus throw, but every athlete scored lifetime bests that day.

I treated the team to a fast-food banquet, and the recollection is among the best memories I have of teaching and coaching at Juan Diego Catholic High School.

It's easy to recruit to a team after an event like that. The athletes became the best ambassadors I could ask for after this meet. Building excellence also breeds an interest in more excellence.

I see results, community involvement and *Don't make look stupid!* as the three looping concepts that make up the core ideas of setting goals and ongoing assessment work over the long term. These three are so intertwined, it's hard to separate them, as in our example where the results and community excitement seem to be one and the same.

When someone asks me about coaching, we can get stuck in that middle bit of goal setting and ongoing assessment. That's fine, by the way. That's the key, the core, for a reason. Goal setting is crucial, and it immediately spurs us into assessment.

But, the looping concepts become one's assistant coaches here: excellent results; a joyful community that enriches and enlarges; and elegance, mastery and grace support the goal-setting better than any magic herb or potion.

Some Givens about Training Systems

As you read books, articles and programs about athletic performance, fitness or health, it's easy to get buried under what seems like massively conflicting information. In pure candor, it's confusing.

Oscar Wilde could easily have been talking about fitness when he wrote, "The test of a first rate intelligence is the ability to hold two opposing ideas in the mind at the same time and still retain the ability to function."

Let's review systems more closely.

We are at a wonderful point in American football where the game is reinventing itself as we watch. When I played, we were chess pieces. We set up, someone moved, we countermoved. Today, there are plays where literally no one on offense (the guys with the ball) knows whether the ball will be run or passed even after the ball has been snapped. The moves and countermoves today are made, figuratively and literally, on the fly.

Leading this renaissance is a football offense called *The System*. Now, I love it, but the genius of *The System* is in tossing out half the learning process and therefore doubling the amount of work done on specifics in the same amount of time. I can't explain it better than what I found on one of my favorite websites, *smartfootball.com*—

> While at Valdosta, they primarily engaged in addition by subtraction. They cut out a few passing plays that weren't as useful, shrank the running game to little more than an "iso" lead play and a draw, and, most famously, made the offense asymmetrical: Instead of running each play in one direction and having "right" and "left" variations on each formation, they made the offense entirely right-handed, always putting the tight-end or "Y" receiver to the right and the split-end or "X" to the left, and only moving "Z" around.

Our original rule number one is good in any system: *addition by subtraction.*

When my young discus throwers go to a track meet, I always have to prep myself for the onslaught of questions upon our return.

"Coach, this guy did this and that guy was doing that. Can we do this?"

"Did you win?"

"Yes."

"Hmmm...let's stick with the boring things we're doing."

My throwing practices are basically the same day in and day out. We have pre-practice drills for fifteen minutes; then we meet and gather as a team. Later, out on the field, the athletes spend about half an hour playing catch using the four-step approach. We then split up the group and work drills in and out of the ring.

In an hour, these throwers average over a hundred throws while the competition often hasn't even gotten to the field yet, as they are still doing jogging, plyos, mobility, flexibility, hurdles, sprints and whatever.

My system? Throwers throw.

The funny thing is this: I used to do everything else, too. I started tossing stuff out—subtracting!—when I realized that discus throwers need to turn, and shot putters need to throw. What began to amaze me is that my throwers began throwing farther and farther by just—wait for it—throwing.

Now, there's nothing wrong with doing all this extra stuff and, honestly, it might help your throwers ultimately throw farther than mine. But how will you know?

You'll observe rule two: *Additional components must improve the overall organism.*

For a fat-loss client, changing from goblet squats to single-side squats might zap off a few extra calories due to inefficient movement for a while, but, honestly, we usually make changes to the program because of boredom.

And, speaking in total candor, combating boredom is perfectly fine and part of the whole process of long-term training.

For your QII person, those in collision sports and occupations, it's true that they need to do a lot of things at a very high level. You're right, of course, but you've forgotten rule number one!

The third and final rule is one that is uncomfortable for many: *The system survives the loss of its founder.*

This might be my religious studies background reaching up from my gut, but the key to long-term success of any good idea is the next person in line. Things grow in interesting ways, both horizontally and vertically.

Let's start with this idea of vertical growth: If I coach you in the discus, I'm going to tell you about Lindsay's last throw in the state meet for the win. I'm going to talk about Eric Lindquist's first-round personal record to win the same meet. I'm going to tell you about Paul Northway throwing the discus into the street at a meet because the field wasn't big enough.

Soon you will hear about all the great Utah State throwers. You'll hear about Coach Maughan and how at the nationals, his competitor gave him a secret to big throws. Coach followed the suggestion and won. Both athletes, for reference, had just returned from fighting in World War II.

I'll expect you to be part of this tradition soon. That's vertical.

A system needs to be able to thrive and survive over time by having a history, a family tree and a story. That's the vertical aspect of growth, and it's part of the survival of the group after the founder dies.

As long as I breathe, the Utah State discus throwing tradition continues. Ideally, I left enough crumbs so others may find that path.

The horizontal aspect is the current community. With a system, we can grow outward and discover, taste and test other ideas, programs and systems. We can stretch out as wide as needed to improve our system. Our vertical axis allows us to test other things and still stay true to the original plan.

My *Intervention* program is based on this idea. It's a system that walks the reader through everything from the original goal through exactly where the person is today, with the gaps and shortcomings highlighted next to those glorious strengths and superpowers. If a person wants to be a thrower, we handle that the same way as those who want to be sprinters or lose a few pounds of body fat.

A system must always be big enough, both vertically and horizontally, to add and subtract—and remember why we did either—when better ways of doing things come along.

Intervention lends itself to a systems approach to training. It strives for simplicity and rewards hard work. It demands a bit of thinking. It also reflects the real world, a person's real life.

Regularly review the way you look at training—and life— through our three rules.

1. Addition by subtraction.

2. Additional components must improve the overall organism.

3. The system survives the loss of its founder.

If you haven't seen the earlier material and would like to learn more, these ideas are fleshed out in the book and DVD called *Intervention,* and in my *Systems Approach* DVD.

Assessing These Rules

Most people have a story about addition by subtraction. In the workplace or at a party, someone might leave, and everything seems to feel better. In my coaching career, eliminating certain kinds of traditional conditioning, especially dreadful things like wind sprints, picked up the rest of the practice period, both emotionally and physically.

Assessing addition by subtraction is usually apparent. There's a feeling of more time magically appearing, and better overall clarity.

Rule number two—additional components must improve the overall organism—is the hardest to assess. When something comes along and you add it, how can you discern whether it's working?

I have a model called *The Two Test Tubes*. One test tube is where you put the new idea, exercise, nutrient, job, relationship or whatever. It's your energy, investment, capital and juju, those good deeds (like over-tipping) that end up rewarding you later in life.

The other test tube is what you get back. It doesn't have to be money, but that's sure a nice measuring stick. It can also be wonderful memories, life-changing moments and "just a lot of fun."

Now, make an imaginary mark at maybe 20 percent of the full test tube. I use that to look at anything I do or add to my system (or life). We're following the Pareto principle with this idea, the 80–20 rule. True, in business this has become a cliché, but it absolutely is a wonderful way to judge things.

I say yes to most opportunities or new ideas. I toss them in and see what happens. Then, I give them a grade.

- **A**—Just like in school, this is the best you can do. If something takes 20 percent of your time or energy and fills that "what you get back" tube 80 percent, you have a winner! When people start doing goblet squats and farmer walks and it rekindles their training, I figure we hand out that A grade. Royalties of all kinds would fit here, too. There is nothing more fun than a check in the mail from something you did ten years ago.

- **B**—This is what you would expect from most things. You put your time in, and you get what you give back. And that's pretty good!

 ♦ **C**—These are those little things that take and give at that 20 percent level. This is fine, but not earth-shattering, and you might find hundreds of these in your life. I still say yes to most opportunities, as there's always a chance something might end up being an A.

 ♦ **F**—When you find something is eating up most of your time and energy and you only get back a fraction of the effort, stop. Stop now.

In training, if you add a new idea from a workshop or article, assess it through this lens. If it takes months or years to learn and master, yet only adds a bit—or worse, pulls you down a notch—you can say it was a failure. Drop it, move on and try not to repeat the mistake in the future.

If, on the other hand, something new is easy to add and it immediately changes lives, you have a rare gem. Give yourself a pat on the back and an A grade.

And for rule number three—truly great systems not only survive the loss of the founder, but thrive and grow after this loss. This growth not only reflects well on the wisdom and insights of the founder, but also on the gifts of the next generation. When looking upon a successful institution, we can see the rings of growth long after the original seed.

This is true in every field, too.

Chapter 12

In Conclusion

That Feedback Loop

Setting goals and doing assessments create a feedback loop similar to a figure eight. During the first moments after asking, "What do you want?" or "What's your goal?," we begin to sift through all the unlimited options that a human has in this millennia.

Finishing the *1-2-3-4 Assessment* gives us another insight on this path: what the client needs to do first and foremost. Immediately addressing those needs might be the ticket to accomplishing the stated goal.

Correctly using the *Five Tools* and taking some time to examine the whole system will keep the client on the road to the goal. As we near it, we find some new challenge, assess again and continue doing this for—literally—the life of the trainee.

The process is simple—

1. Do what is needed.

2. Follow an appropriate program.

3. Finish the program!

4. Reassess.

Generally, the program will look something like this—

♦ Stretch what is tightening—pecs, biceps, hip flexors, hamstrings.

♦ Strengthen what is weakening—glutes, abs, delts, triceps.

♦ Eat like an adult.

♦ Seek mastery.

I finished my book *Intervention* with the following sentence:

"Let success happen."

There is no one more successful than the person striving for a worthy goal.

Good luck as you guide your clients on this journey.

Appendices

Appendix 1

Suggestions for Further Reading and Review

I'VE FILMED A LINEUP OF VIDEOS to demonstrate the exercises discussed in this book and to describe some of the concepts. You'll find the full collection at *danjohn.net/can-you-go*.

If you're new to my work, *Intervention* can be considered a companion book to *Can you go? Intervention* is a much deeper look at appropriate exercise selection and programming for advanced athletes, but shares the need to make use of foresight and planning in overall training.

For the exercises mentioned in this book, there are two books that blend the same overall philosophy—

- ♦ Pat Flynn's book *Paleo Workouts for Dummies* (yes, the title needs "something") is a great reference for the fundamental human movements.

♦ Brett Turley's book *The Minimalism Effect: Become Injury Free, Build Amazing Movement and Strength by Doing Less,* provides us with the same family of exercises, but with more attention to regressions and progressions.

Pat and Brett will give some clarity to my meager attention to exercise detail.

Denise Minger's book *Death by Food Pyramid* is the clearest explanation of finding an intelligent solution to our modern eating problem. If you've ever been confused when you heard that a food or diet is "good" or "bad" in the same month, this book will provide some helpful guidance.

Dan Millman's book *Way of the Peaceful Warrior* is filled with moments of clarity for the coach and athlete. I can't think of another book that redefines the role of sport in life better than his work.

Appendix **2**

Programming for Everybody Else
(Ones through Sevens) and the Active Athlete

I GET ASKED THIS question a lot—

> "Can you simplify the programming
> of *Ones* through *Sevens*?"

Even after I cover the question, it comes up again during workshops. Many struggle with grasping the three circles of *Body Comp, Strength, Mobility,* and understanding how to apply the "answer" to the client's needs.

So, memorize this: *Focus on what the clients need, not what they want.*

Now, as a good salesperson, you will quickly suggest the idea that what the clients need is also what they want, but let's get back to the question.

Ones—these clients passed the plank and the waist-to-height measurement test. The experience of the past sixty-plus years of physical culture teaches us that hypertrophy and mobility work are going to work best for these people. Janda taught us, basically, to strengthen the glutes, the delts, the triceps and the ab wall. As I learned from the 100-Pound Club, squats and presses are going to do wonders here. On the mobility side, keep it simple at first, and stretch the pecs, the biceps, the hip flexors and the hamstrings.

In a way, it would be wonderful to be a *One.* Goblet squats followed by the hip flexor stretch, and then some presses mixed with something like the sun salutation from yoga is a pretty nice combination workout.

The *Twos* can follow this same protocol, but they will also need some nutrition advice and inefficient exercise. Hopping on an exercycle during rest periods between the lifting program of the *Ones* or adding kettlebell swings might do the trick.

For eating, food prep is the key. To begin, buy canned vegetables with the pop-top lid, or get those precut packages and up the intake. My local store has a mixed bag with eight different vegetables in a size that's perfect for anything from omelets to soups and stews.

The *Three* client's road is pretty simple: food preparation and moving around more. This is the whole *eat less, move more* philosophy that's so simple to type and so difficult to pursue. That's why I like group challenges to use the power of community to support fat-loss goals. Send these clients into a 10,000-swing challenge or a jogging, cycling or rowing club with weekly events. I know, easy to say…hard to do.

So, let's change "Eat less, move more" to "Prep more food, train alone less often."

The *Four* client is very common among women. For them, we want to make the training supportive of some women's fear of weights. Trust me, to look massive and huge is a task worthy of a ballad or epic. It is far, far harder than anything they can imagine.

This is why I'm a fan of combining kettlebell and barbell work for the *Fours.* Kettlebells certainly can be used for building strength, but they also make us sweat doing swings and snatches. Barbell work provides the best feedback in the world: Almost every workout in the beginning allows us to add more plates...a good thing!

The pure *Five* client is easy: fundamental human movements with appropriate reps and sets. Just remember to spend a little time reviewing the Goldilocks concept, and just get stronger over time.

I wish it could be fancier, but that's what the *Five* needs.

For the *Six* client, and those who "passed" all the tests, we mix mobility and strength work, and they can do those "fun" workouts like the hypertrophy and mobility workout on page 187.

Moreover, with good coaching, equipment and facilities, the *Sixes* can explore the Olympic lifts and the powerlifts. I'm a huge fan of the O lifts at the proper time and proper place in a training career.

The key to coaching *Sevens* is mental state. Focus on the tiny habits, and gather the benefits of little things like drinking more water and going for a daily walk. Over time, push the *Sevens* into strength, mobility, hypertrophy and inefficient exercise, but first... keep them coming back.

Of all the aspects of strength coaching, the most difficult is programming. It's difficult to program beyond a few days due to life issues, injuries, illness and that something that came up.

So, I want to offer a few general programs that take us from the general to the specific, and you find those in the following appendices.

The first is a simple ten-exercise program that covers every quality and seems to be repeatable and doable for most people. This is a four-week training program that attempts to address nearly every quality the typical client needs to work on. You'll find this beginning on page 161.

Expanding on the variation of movements, the next program, which starts on page 177, is a weekly template. *The Basic Weekly Training Template: Basic Training for the Seasoned Trainee* demands a fair amount of equipment and exercise choices. It's a program that would be excellent for someone who wanted to drastically improve fitness for an upcoming event. It works well for both sports and the beach, by the way.

Next, we look at a program focused on building muscle—hypertrophy—while striving to retain mobility. If there is a Holy Grail in fitness, it would be a program that increases lean body mass and holds onto mobility and flexibility. This program, see page 187, is my contribution. Not as complex as *The Basic Weekly Training Template: Basic Training for the Seasoned Trainee,* this program focuses on an intelligent approach to increasing load.

The next program is a last-minute training program for a pair of climbers who were offered the opportunity of a lifetime and took it. Many people ask me how one gears up for an event, and this day by day, week by week program will give some insights into how we both physically and mentally prepare for the challenge. This program is outlined in Appendix 6, page 191.

Finally, I share an advanced program I use for college throwers. This program assumes we're working with someone well versed in all the disciplines of weightlifting, and who also has a level of mastery in the sport. It seems so simple on paper, but it should give you some ideas for training the active athlete. Look for this one beginning on page 223.

Let's dive into programming.

Appendix 3

Classic Conditioning in X Moves: A Monthly Training Program in Ten Movements

NOT LONG AGO, I was asked if I could provide a full training program including strength, cardio, mobility and flexibility with only ten movements.

I like that kind of question. When I'm trying to get a sports coach to embrace more simplicity, I often ask a simple question, "If, for whatever reason, you could only train for three fifteen-minute sessions a week, what would you do?"

The following is my attempt to answer that question. It is a very simple plan based on ten movements. It respects the insights of DeLorme and Watkins. You'll see strength and hypertrophy work founded on their basic program. Janda's work is reflected here, too, as the program is glute-focused each day, stretching

161

what needs to be stretched and strengthening what needs to be strengthened.

To these, I added the Tabata protocol twice a month. For mobility and tonic workouts—tonic workouts are those light, refreshing training sessions that seem to undo the soreness of a tough training session—I kept the basics, but tried to vary the reps and load a bit.

It's simple stuff, and nothing I've included is original. The goal is to follow the plan and strive for mastery, beauty and elegance in the training sessions. This kind of programming is excellent for anyone over about twenty-eight, or anyone looking for an uncomplicated approach to full-body training.

Here are the basic ideas we honor—

1. Advanced programming that includes mobility, stability, core work, intervals, strength training and cardio can be done with a minimum of equipment and movements.

2. By planning a month, or two, or three at a time, it's possible to build in days that focus on one tool or another.

3. It's always better to have a few movements that cover a lot of needs, rather than to have dozens of isolated bits.

And the ten movements are—

1. One-Arm Press
2. One-Arm Row
3. Swing
4. Goblet Squat
5. Bird Dog
6. Push-Up Position Plank (PUPP)

7. Hip-Flexor Stretch

8. Hip-Flexor Rainbow

9. Six-Point Zenith

10. Suitcase Carry

I've demonstrated and explained all the movements in recent videos, which you'll find at danjohn.net/can-you-go.

Loading for the Program

Light—50%
Medium—75%
Heavy—100%

For this program, the weight is based on what the person can do for ten repetitions, not for a single lift. This will be a load that can be done sometimes for eight reps, and sometimes for twelve. You'll see the *Light-Medium-Heavy* references in the programs that follow.

Lifts should never be missed.

Progression or Regression—Adjusting the Weight

Recently, Bryan Mann from the University of Missouri did an interesting study on using the DeLorme and Watkins protocol. The previous workout was based on their insights of training, the 10-5-10 on the strength movements. His insight on a standardized progression was very helpful, as well as was the fact that he proved that the old-school methods still work. You can use the following general template to adjust the load for future training sessions.

Based on the number of reps completed for set number three, reduce, maintain or increase as follows—

> **4–5 reps:** *Reduce the weight by 5 to 10 pounds next time*
> **6–8 reps:** *Maintain weight or reduce by 5 pounds next time*
> **8–12 reps:** *Maintain weight next time*
> **12–15 reps:** *Increase the weight by 5 to 10 pounds next time*
> **15+ reps:** *Increase the weight by 10 to 15 pounds next time*

If your client only gets to 0–3 reps on the heavy set, you either overshot the weight estimate, or there's something else going on. When the numbers for each of the third sets put the client in different categories (for example, 7, 9, 12, and 15), you may need to make an educated estimate for the next session.

Program A: Simple Strength

Getting stronger is the foundation of all fitness goals. Brett Jones put it this way: "Absolute strength is the glass. Everything else is the liquid inside the glass. The bigger the glass, the more of everything else you can do."

Strive to increase the weights over time. Stretching during rest periods keeps the intensity and heart rate up.

Push

One-Arm Press

- 10 reps, light weight
  with Hip-Flexor Stretch, Right Knee Down

- 5 reps, medium weight
  with Hip-Flexor Stretch, Left Knee Down

- 10 reps, heavy weight

Pull

One-Arm Row

+ 10 reps, light weight
  with Hip-Flexor Rainbow, Right Knee Down

+ 5 reps, medium weight
  with Hip-Flexor Rainbow, Left Knee Down

+ 10 reps, heavy weight

Hinge

Swing

+ 30 reps, light weight
  with Bird Dog, Right Knee Down

+ 15 reps, medium weight
  with Bird Dog, Left Knee Down

+ 30 reps, heavy weight

Squat

Goblet Squat

+ 10 reps, light weight
  with Six-Point Zenith, Right Hand Sweeps Up

+ 5 reps, medium weight
  with Six-Point Zenith, Left Hand Sweeps Up

+ 10 reps, heavy weight

Can You Go?

Plank
Pushup-Position Plank

- Two minutes

Carry
Suitcase Carry

- With the less-dominant hand, walk as far as you can under load. Put the weight down. Turn around, grab the weight and come back with the dominant hand.

Program B: The Cardio Hit Workout

Mixing the dynamic swing with the grinding squat is an interesting way to increase heart rate. Adding a stretch between sets will keep the heart rate high and will also add some heart rate variability—a good thing. Don't have clients hold the stretches for more than thirty seconds; they should quickly pop up for another set of swings.

- 15 Swings; 1 Goblet Squat
  with Hip-Flexor Stretch, Right Knee Down

- 15 Swings; 1 Goblet Squat
  with Hip-Flexor Stretch, Left Knee Down

- 15 Swings; 1 Goblet Squat
  with Hip-Flexor Rainbow, Right Knee Down

- 15 Swings; 1 Goblet Squat
  with Hip-Flexor Rainbow, Left Knee Down

- 15 Swings; 1 Goblet Squat
  with Bird Dog, Right Knee Down

- 15 Swings; 1 Goblet Squat
  with Bird Dog, Left Knee Down

- 15 Swings; 1 Goblet Squat
  with Six-Point Zenith, Right Hand Sweeps Up

- 15 Swings; 1 Goblet Squat
  with Six-Point Zenith, Left Hand Sweeps Up

- 15 Swings; 1 Goblet Squat
  with Pushup-Position Plank

- 15 Swings; 1 Goblet Squat
  with Suitcase Walk, Right and Left

Program C: Tonic Recharge Workout

This is the workout to do following a Tabata day. It's an easy day, but still, always focus on the long-term goal...and the journey.

Push

One-Arm Press

- 10 reps, light weight
  with Hip-Flexor Stretch, Right Knee Down
  with Hip-Flexor Stretch, Left Knee Down

Pull

One-Arm Row

- 10 reps, light weight
  with Hip-Flexor Rainbow, Right Knee Down
  with Hip-Flexor Rainbow, Left Knee Down

Hinge

Swing

- ♦ 30 reps, light weight
    with Bird Dog, Right Knee Down
    with Bird Dog, Left Knee Down

Squat

Goblet Squat

- ♦ 10 reps, light weight
    with Six-Point Zenith, Right Hand Sweeps Up
    with Six-Point Zenith, Left Hand Sweeps Up

Plank

Pushup-Position Plank

- ♦ 1 minute

Program D: Bimonthly Tabata

We only use a ten-second rest, so alert your client to be ready to go again at seven seconds. Please use a Tabata timer, available for free on the web.

We go for twenty seconds, rest for ten and then repeat another seven times for a total of eight rounds—just four minutes of working out. Stay focused.

Tabata Workout One

- ♦ Tabata Goblet Squats for 4 minutes

Tabata Workout Two

- ♦ Tabata Swings for 4 minutes

Program E: The Mobility Workout

If the client is under thirty years of age, go through the movements for two circuits—do every movement once, finish the list and repeat.

For clients from thirty to fifty years of age: Go through the movements for three circuits.

For clients over fifty years of age: Go for at least three circuits, but strive to do four or five.

For every lift or stretch—

♦ Hold each position for thirty seconds.

♦ Make sure the feet are grounded: Stretch out the toes and grab the ground while driving the heels down.

♦ Whenever standing, attempt to ensure the beltline is parallel with the floor. Squeeze the glutes to do this. Under load, you may notice the tummy pooch out a bit; this is fine.

♦ Be sure to breathe! Mastery of the breath is one of the secrets to super strength.

The movements, which you'll recognize by now, are—

♦ Hip-Flexor Stretch, Right Knee Down

♦ Hip-Flexor Stretch, Left Knee Down

♦ Hip-Flexor Rainbow, Right Knee Down

♦ Hip-Flexor Rainbow, Left Knee Down

♦ Bird Dog, Right Knee Down

♦ Bird Dog, Left Knee Down

♦ Six-Point Zenith, Right Hand Sweeps Up

♦ Six-Point Zenith, Left Hand Sweeps Up

Tips to the Movements

One-Arm Press

♦ Use both hands to set the weight in place on the shoulder.

♦ Squeeze your glutes first, then begin the rep.

♦ Strive to have the elbow in a vertical line under the wrist throughout the movement.

♦ Finish with the beltline parallel to the floor.

One-Arm Row

♦ The nonworking arm should be securely locked onto the off leg.

♦ Hold the thumb of the working arm in the armpit for a short pause on every rep.

♦ Do not jerk the weight. Move the weight under control, and drive the elbow to the ceiling.

Swing

♦ At the top of the movement, find the plank position: glutes tight, thighs tight and upper body tight. This is where we drive the weight back to the hinge.

♦ Feel the hinge in your hamstrings. Think of the position of snapping a football back to a punter.

Goblet Squat

- Begin the movement with the glutes locked and the beltline parallel to the floor.

- Drop the body between the legs, and strive to push the knees out with the elbows.

- Pause.

- Squeeze the thighs to return to the standing position.

Bird Dog

- If the left knee is down, strive to drive the heel of the right foot straight back.

- Try to have both butt cheeks on the same plane, parallel to the floor.

- Hold this position for as long as you can.

- If you go over two minutes, pump the left elbow to the right knee for reps.

- Switch sides.

Pushup-Position Plank (PUPP)

- Squeeze the glutes.

- Try to squeeze "the heads of trolls" in your armpits.

- Hold this for up to two minutes.

- Focus on squeezing, not just surviving the time.

Can You Go?

Planks (Variation)

- Same as the PUPP, but on the elbows.

- Try to pull the elbows to the knees the entire time.

Hip-Flexor Stretch

- If the left knee is down, make sure the right big toe is pushing hard into the ground.

- Squeeze the glutes, and pull the top of the head to Zenith.

- Feel the stretch in the front of the left hip.

- Switch sides.

Hip-Flexor Rainbow

- We begin in the same position as the hip-flexor stretch, but with the left knee down.

- Sweep the right arm in a long, slow arc from overhead to straight back, trying to open up the chest and core.

- Bonus points: Close your right eye and try to trace the movement with your left eye.

Six-Point Zenith

- On your hands, knees and feet, use your right arm to hug your left knee.

- In a long, lazy arc, stretch the right arm up to Zenith, or as close as you can.

- Use the same reach as with the hip-flexor rainbow.

- Feel the stretch in your chest and core, and continue to hug and stretch.

- Bonus points: Close your right eye try to trace the movement with your left eye.

Suitcase Carry

- Pick up a weight in one hand.

- Stand tall, ensure your beltline is parallel to the floor and walk.

- Repeat with the other side.

Here's a table outlining a month's layout of the programs described above.

Sunday	Monday	Tuesday	Wednesday	Thursday	Friday	Saturday
Rest	Program A *Simple*	Program E *Mobility*	Program B *Cardio*	Rest	Program A *Simple*	Program D-1 *Goblet Squats*
Rest	Program C *Tonic*	Program E *Mobility*	Program A *Simple*	Rest	Program B *Cardio*	Program A *Simple*
Rest	Program A *Simple*	Program E *Mobility*	Program B *Cardio*	Rest	Program A *Simple*	Program D-2 *Swings*
Rest	Program C *Tonic*	Program E *Mobility*	Program A *Simple*	Rest	Program B *Cardio*	Program A *Simple*

This is a nice way of looping the workouts together. Having one day a week—Tuesday in this example—to do just mobility work is a nice way to keep a program fresh. Note that we do the simple strength twice a week and six cardio workouts a month.

Most people need to improve their strength and hypertrophy, and I found the Tabatas to do a lot for lean body mass.

I like having two days off a week to enjoy life, but it ends up being more like three or four, as the mobility and tonic workouts are just not very hard.

Don't ignore the tonic workouts. Many people err by missing a chance to move and refresh. It's part of an intelligent, long-term approach to training, but many wrongly ignore the tonic workouts that are the "hair of the dog that bit you."

Teaching This Workout

My favorite way to teach new movements is to get the group in a circle if possible, and lead them through a workout. As the movements are explained, new members can listen and watch and practice as the experienced people model proper movement.

This way of teaching originated with the Coyote Point Kettlebell Club, and we retain its memory whenever we add or develop a new drill, regression or progression.

In this program, we add high-knee marching in place for most of the segments. Marching in place is a nice counterbalance to the swings and squats.

Here's an example of a workout in this program.

Coyote Point Kettlebell Club Workout

+ 10 Swings; 1 Goblet Squat; March in Place
  with Six-Point Zenith, left hand high

+ 10 Swings; 1 Goblet Squat; March in Place
  with Six-Point Zenith, right hand high

+ 10 Swings; 1 Goblet Squat; March in Place
  with One-Arm Press, left knee down

- 10 Swings; 1 Goblet Squat; March in Place
  with Hip-Flexor Stretch, left knee down

- 10 Swings; 1 Goblet Squat; March in Place
  with One-Arm Press, right knee down

- 10 Swings; 1 Goblet Squat; March in Place
  with Hip-Flexor Stretch, right knee down

- 10 Swings; 1 Goblet Squat; March in Place
  with One-Arm Row, left hand

- 10 Swings; 1 Goblet Squat; March in Place
  with Hip-Flexor Rainbow, left knee down

- 10 Swings; 1 Goblet Squat; March in Place
  with One-Arm Row, right hand

- 10 Swings; 1 Goblet Squat; March in Place
  with Hip-Flexor Rainbow, right knee down

- 10 Swings; 1 Goblet Squat; March in Place
  with Hip-Flexor Stretch, left knee down

- 10 Swings; 1 Goblet Squat; March in Place
  with Hip-Flexor Stretch, right knee down

- 10 Swings; 1 Goblet Squat; March in Place
  with Bird Dog, left knee down

- 10 Swing; 1 Goblet Squat; March in Place
  with Bird Dog, right knee down

- 10 Swings; 1 Goblet Squat; March in Place
  with One-Arm Press, left knee down

- 10 Swings; 1 Goblet Squat; March in Place
  with One-Arm Press, right knee down

- 10 Swings; 1 Goblet Squat; March in Place
  with One-Arm Row, left hand

- 10 Swings; 1 Goblet Squat; March in Place
  with One-Arm Row, right hand

- 10 Swing; 1 Goblet Squat; March in Place
  with Bird Dog, left knee down

- 10 Swing; 1 Goblet Squat; March in Place
  with Bird Dog, right knee down

- 10 Swings; 1 Goblet Squat
  with 5 Proper Pushups

- 10 Swings; 1 Goblet Squat
  with 4 Proper Pushups

- 10 Swings; 1 Goblet Squat
  with 3 Proper Pushups

- 10 Swings; 1 Goblet Squat
  with 2 Proper Pushups

- 10 Swing; 1 Goblet Squat
  with 1 Proper Pushup

This is 250 swings, 25 squats and 15 pushups.

You'll see that we've also added proper pushups. If you don't know them, here's the technique. When you come to the ground, put your chest fully on the ground, release both hands off the ground, and send them sideways into a T position. Return the hands to central and push back up. That's one proper pushup.

Appendix **4**

The Basic Weekly Training Template: Basic Training for the Seasoned Trainee

HERE'S AN EXAMPLE OF THE three principles of *Movement first*, *If it's important do it every day* and *Repeat, repeat, repeat* in action. Here we're looking for a focused hinge and squat day on Monday, and a pull-centric day on Tuesday, which are countered by a heavy pressing day on Thursday and, as we gear up for the weekend, loaded carries on Friday. Yet, on each day, this workout adds a little of the other movements.

This workout involves a lot of repetitions. The load will make this workout harder, and this would be a more advanced program than *Classic Conditioning in Ten Movements,* as we're asking for more variety in training.

Daily Warmup

- Groundwork (rolling on the ground)

- 15 Hinge Movements, 5 Goblet Squats, then March in Place

- Full-Body Stretch

- 15 Hinge Movements, 4 Goblet Squats, then March in Place

- T-Spine Mobility Work

- 15 Hinge Movements, 3 Goblet Squats, then March in Place

- Groundwork (rolling on the ground)

- 15 Hinge Movements, 2 Goblet Squats, then March in Place

- Full-Body Stretch

- 15 Hinge Movements, 1 Goblet Squat, then March in Place

- T-Spine Mobility Work

Subtotal: 75 Hinges and 15 Squats, and a lot of marching, stretching and rolling around

MONDAY

Daily warmup (above), then—

The Workout

Two times through these five movements, in a loop

1. 25 Hinge Movements
2. 5 Squat Movements
3. 15 Hinge Movements
4. Mini-Band Walk
5. Farmer Walk

Next, do this superset, back and forth between the two movements

Pullups: 3-2-2-2-1
One-Arm Presses: 1-1-1-1-1

Two times through the following superset

25 Pulling Movements
5 Ab Wheels

Five times through this triset, looping through all three movements

25 Hinge Movements
10 Standing Hinge Movements
1 Goblet Squat

Monday Workout Total

Push: 5
Pull: 60
Hinge: 230
Squat: 30
Loaded Carries: 2 Variations
Sixth Movement Groundwork: 4

Can You Go?

TUESDAY
Daily warmup (above), then—

The Workout
Three times through the following superset

> 24 Pulling Movements (3 variations of 8 reps)
> 5 Ab Wheels

Next, in a superset, back and forth between the two movements

> Pullups: 3-3-2-2-1
> One-Arm Presses: 2-1-1-1-1

Three times through the following loop

> 15 TRX Biceps Curls
> 15 TRX Triceps Extensions

Finally, 2 Bear Crawl–Bear Hug with Heavy Bags

Tuesday Workout Total
Push: 6 (45 extensions)
Pull: 83
Hinge: 125
Squat: 15
Loaded Carry: 2 Variations
Sixth Movements: 4

THURSDAY
Daily warmup (above), then—

The Workout

Do these in a superset, back and forth between the two movements

Pullups: 3-3-3-2-1
One-Arm Presses: 2-2-1-1-1

Three times through these two movements
Double Presses*: 2-3-5-10
Stretch

* Round One: Light Double Presses
Round Two: Heavy Double Presses
Round Three: Medium Double Presses

Three times through in a loop
25 Hip Thrusts
10 Goblet Squats
Suitcase Carry

Thursday Workout Total

Push: 67
Pull: 12
Hinge: 200
Squat: 45
Loaded Carry: 1 Variation
Sixth Movements: 4

FRIDAY

Daily warmup (above), then—

The Workout

Do these in a superset, back and forth between the two movements

Pullups: 1-1-1
One-Arm Presses: 1-1-1

One time through the following—

- ♦ Mini-Band Walk with Black Band (hard)
- ♦ 3 Squat Variations
- ♦ Waiter Walk
- ♦ 3 Squat Variations
- ♦ Farmer Walk
- ♦ 3 Squat Variations
- ♦ Light Bag Carry
- ♦ 3 Squat Variations
- ♦ Medium Bag Carry
- ♦ 3 Squat Variations
- ♦ Heavy Bag Carry
- ♦ 3 Squat Variations

Two times through these four, in a loop

15 TRX Triceps Extensions
15 TRX Biceps Curls

15 French Presses

15 Barbell Curls

Friday Workout Total

Push: 3 (plus 30 extensions)

Pull: 3

Hinge: 75

Squat: 33

Loaded Carry: 6 Variations

Sixth Movements: 2

Weekly Totals

Push: 81 (plus all extensions)

Pull: 158

Hinge: 605

Squat: 123

Loaded Carries: 11 Variations

Sixth Movements: 14 Variations

Exercise Selection

See me demonstrate these at danjohn.net/can-you-go.

Groundwork

- ♦ Turkish Getup

- ♦ Naked Turkish Getup

- ♦ Basic Bodyweight Training

- ♦ Foam Rolling (and the like)

- ♦ Rolling on the Ground

Can You Go?

Hinge Movements

- Swing

- Bulgarian Goat Bag Swing

- Stop and Pop, or Naked Swing

Goblet Squat

- Goblet Squat Regression
  - Potato Sack Squat
  - Doorknob Drill
  - Six-Point Rock

Full-Body Stretch

- Sun Salute (Yoga)

- Stoney Stretch

T-Spine Mobility Work

- Windmill

- Windmill Stick

- Six-Point Zenith Stretch

Hinge Movements on Floor

- Hip Thrust
- Supine Bridge Plank

Pulling Movements

- Barbell Row

- Dumbbell Row

- TRX T-Y-I

- TRX Row

Presses

- Overhead Press

- Bench Press

- Double-Kettlebell Press

- Single Press

Don't worry about the names of the exercises. There are dozens of books and internet sites that will explain (for better or worse) these particular moves, and I'll demonstrate them for you at *danjohn.net/can-you-go*. The idea here is to follow the principles.

Appendix **5**

Hypertrophy and Mobility Complex

THIS IS A GOOD PROGRAM for both *Sixes* and people who passed all three tests—the 2:1 waist-to-height measurement, the pillow question and the plank. The exercises are discussed and demonstrated in the videos you'll find at *danjohn.net/can-you-go*.

This workout is designed to be repeated, and the load increases by the standards of DeLorme and Mann, as described earlier on page 163.

Cluster One

- One-Hand Press: 10 reps per hand at 50% of 10RM
- Windmill Stick
- Six-Point Rocks and Nods (from *Pressing Reset,* by Tim Anderson)

- One-Hand Press: 5 reps per hand at 75% of 10RM
- Windmill Stick
- Six-Point Rocks and Nods

- One-Hand Press: 10 reps per hand at 100% of 10RM
- Windmill Stick
- Six-Point Rocks and Nods

Cluster Two

- Front Squat: 10 reps at 50% of 10RM
- 20 Hip Thrusts
- 15 Swings

- Front Squat: 5 reps at 75% of 10RM
- 20 Hip Thrusts
- 15 Swings

- Front Squat: 10 reps at 100% of 10RM
- 20 Hip Thrusts
- 15 Swings

Cluster Three

- 10 TRX T Pulls
- Stoney Stretch
- Three-Point Bird Dog

- 5 TRX T Pulls
- Stoney Stretch
- Three-Point Bird Dog

- 15 TRX T Pulls
- Stoney Stretch
- Three-Point Bird Dog

*Don't worry about load with TRX work.

Cluster Four

+ 30 Swings with a Light Load
+ 15 TRX Biceps Curls
+ Single-Side Bird Dog

+ 15 Swings with a Medium Load
+ 15 TRX Biceps Curls
+ Single-Side Bird Dog

+ 30 Swings with a Heavy Load
+ 15 TRX Biceps Curls
+ Single-Side Bird Dog

*Add any kind of loaded carry to finish.

Climb Every Mountain: Six Weeks of Prep for the Tallest Mountain on a Continent

NOT LONG AGO, I WAS ASKED to apply my principles toward last-minute training for a mountain climb. On the list of things to say, "last minute" and "mountain climb" shouldn't be together, but the people involved needed help.

Not only did they survive the climb, they thrived. Some of the drills need some teaching, which you'll find at *danjohn.net/can-you-go,* but look at the general picture here.

Daily Warmup
- Naked Turkish Getup
- Windmill Stick
- Hip-Flexor Stretch
- Elevated Rolls

For the elevated rolls, start in the pushup-position plank. Raise the sole of the right foot as high as you can, then reach across the left leg. Try to hold the hands down, and put the right foot left of the down foot. Release the right hand and point it to Zenith. It doesn't matter how you return to the PUPP, but once you get back there, repeat on the other side.

Kettlebell Work

- One-Arm Press
  For load, pick a bell you can do for five to eight reps.

- Swing
  Men: 24 or 32 (kilos)
  Women: 16 or 20/24

- Goblet Squat
  Men: 24 or 32
  Women: 16 or 20/24

TRX or Suspension Trainer

- T Pulls

Mini-Bands

- Lateral Walk
  Put the mini-band around the ankles (socks really help) and side-step—feet together, right foot reaches and steps right, left foot follows. Repeat until you hate me.

Loaded Carries with Kettlebells

+ See-Saw Press Walk

    With two kettlebells, alternate pressing with each step. Although you will naturally move to contra-lateral, don't worry at first. Step and press one bell, step and press the other—for distance.

    Men: 16s or 20/24s
    Women: 10s or 12s

+ Farmer Walk

    Two bells, one in each hand, for distance or time

    Men: 24s or 32s
    Women: 16s or 20/24s

+ Suitcase Carry

    One bell in the suitcase position, for distance or time

    Men: 24 or 32
    Women: 16 or 20/24

+ Carrying Judy

    Judy was a woman who wasn't nice, and I named this after her. Get a duffel bag and fill it with one, two or three plastic water softener salt bags. These are about forty pounds. Pick Judy up and carry her away.

+ Bear Hug Carry

    For time or distance

♦ Bear Crawl

Drop onto all fours with hands directly under the shoulders; then rise up onto your feet. Now you're in the bear position! Here you can move forward and backward more quickly than in a standard crawl, and you'll work every major muscle group in the process.

Sprinting

Always start slow and ease up. If you are going to sprint, let your stride and speed slowly increase. Then, go faster, and then ease, ease, ease up. A hundred-yard sprint will only be about twenty to forty yards of sprinting.

Long Easy Walks with a Backpack

We always do these with a heart rate monitor. The load should be based on heart rate—let's just use 145–150 as the HR we want to be the max for the walk. Lower is even better, by the way. Think about it this way: 145–150 means to stop, take the weight off and rest. In fact, I'd prefer 120–130.

Walk for at least ten minutes before judging the load. At my house, we have people loop around the block a few times, and at the finish we just put the load in the garage. Load is kettlebells or dumbbells or plates or bricks or whatever you have around. Kids work fine, too.

Always strive for a quiet head, efficient movements and sense of calm while training.

WEEK ONE (ORIENTATION WEEK)

Week One, Day One

♦ Daily Warmup

5 Minutes of Naked Turkish Getups

A few rounds of—
- Windmill Stick
- Hip-Flexor Stretch
- Elevated Roll

♦ Strength Training Workout
Finish each exercise before moving on to the next—these are not supersets.

One-Arm Press
- 1-2-3-1-2-3 (These are rep counts.)
- Alternate arms. I suggest using the non-dominant hand first, then the dominate one. This means I'd do one press on the left hand, one press right. Then two left, two right, and so on.

25 TRX T Pulls

Goblet Squat
- 2-3-5-2-3-5

75 Swings

Suitcase Carry
- 15 seconds left; 15 seconds right, then 30 seconds L/R, then 45 seconds L/R

Bear Crawl
- 15 minutes
- Explore the movement

Easy Walk
- 15 minutes

Tip: Even if your goal is to prepare for something different, trust me on this: If you get stronger, almost universally, you'll find the path to your goals is easier.

Week One, Day Two

♦ Daily Warmup

5 Minutes of Naked Turkish Getups

A few rounds of—
- Windmill Stick
- Hip-Flexor Stretch
- Elevated Roll
- Lateral Walk with a Mini-Band

♦ Decide on the backpack load today. I'm suggesting around twenty-five to thirty-five pounds—after all, that's been the tradition since the Romans. If the heart rate is through the roof with, say, thirty pounds, we need to adjust this a lot. If the time is available, try to stroll over an hour with the load.

Week One, Day Three

- ◆ Daily Warmup

    5 Minutes of Naked Turkish Getups

    A few rounds of—
    - Windmill Stick
    - Hip-Flexor Stretch
    - Elevated Roll

- ◆ Strength Training Workout

    See-Saw Press Walk
    - 10 seconds; 10 seconds; 10 seconds

    15 TRX T Pulls

    Goblet Squat
    - 1-2-3-1-2-3

    Swings
    - 5 sets of 15

    Judy Bear Hug Walk
    - Determine the load. Add the forty and walk with Judy with both arms around her in the front of the body. Then, try two and then three bags. We want to be able to walk about sixty feet, turn around and walk back. That would be one loop.
    - With an appropriate load, do three single loops: 1-1-1

Week One, Day Four

- ◆ Daily Warmup

  5 Minutes of Naked Turkish Getups

  A few rounds of—
  - Windmill Stick
  - Hip-Flexor Stretch
  - Elevated Roll

- ◆ Sprinting
  - One lap walking (four hundred meters), followed by sprinting one hundred meters. Remember to ease into the sprint, and ease out of it. When you come to a complete slow down, walk another lap. When you finish the lap, sprint another hundred meters (a quarter of the track).
  - Repeat this a total of four times, for a total of five laps. We'll call these "4/1s" for reference. This was 4 x 4/1.

Week One, Day Five

- ◆ Daily Warmup

  5 Minutes of Naked Turkish Getups

  A few rounds of—
  - Windmill Stick
  - Hip-Flexor Stretch
  - Elevated Roll

+ Strength Training

  One-Arm Press
  - 1-2-3-1-2-3

  15 TRX T Pulls

+ Conditioning Workout

  10 Swings, then 5 Goblet Squats

  10 Swings, then 4 Goblet Squats

  10 Swings, then 3 Goblet Squats

  10 Swings, then 2 Goblet Squats

  10 Swings, then 1 Goblet Squat

  Farmer Walk
  - 30 seconds; 30 seconds; 30 seconds

  Backpack Walk
  - Take a short little excursion with the back-pack. Go fifteen minutes to as much as an hour, but don't push it.

Week One, Days Six and Seven

Rest for two days. It doesn't matter which days—it can be Saturday and Sunday, or Thursday and Sunday, or whatever. On the rest days, though, I really want at least a half-hour walk, unloaded...a bit of a stroll. This is important every week.

WEEK TWO

Week Two, Day One

- ◆ Daily Warmup

    5 Minutes of Naked Turkish Getups

    A few rounds of—
    - Windmill Stick
    - Hip-Flexor Stretch
    - Elevated Roll

- ◆ Strength Training Workout

    One-Arm Press
    - 1-2-3-1-2-3

    25 TRX T Pulls

    Goblet Squat
    - 2-3-5-2-3-5

    75 Swings
    - 5 sets of 15

    Suitcase Carry
    - 15 seconds L/R; 30 seconds L/R; 45 seconds L/R; 15 seconds L/R

    Bear Crawls
    - 15 minutes

    Easy Walk
    - 30 minutes

Week Two, Day Two

♦ Daily Warmup

5 Minutes of Naked Turkish Getups

A few rounds of—
- Windmill Stick
- Hip-Flexor Stretch
- Elevated Roll

Lateral Walk with a Mini-Band
- 30 seconds L/R; 30 seconds L/R; 30 seconds L/R

Backpack Walk
- Again, strive for over an hour on this. Consider going longer this week and next week, but if you can't get the time in, that's fine. Either this week or next week, try to get two loaded walks in one day—ideally, an hour for both walks. Have some time between the two so it feels a touch sore to put the backpack back on your back. I can't emphasize the importance of reloading a few times during the training process.

Week Two, Day Three

♦ Daily Warmup

5 Minutes of Naked Turkish Getups

A few rounds of—
- Windmill Stick
- Hip-Flexor Stretch
- Elevated Roll

♦ Strength Training Workout

See-Saw Press Walk
- 10 seconds; 15 seconds; 10 seconds

15 TRX T Pulls

Goblet Squat
- 1-2-3-1-2-3

75 Swings
- 5 sets of 15

Judy Bear Hug Walk
- 1-2-1 loops

Week Two, Day Four

♦ Daily Warmup

5 Minutes of Naked Turkish Getups

A few rounds of—
- Windmill Stick
- Hip-Flexor Stretch
- Elevated Roll

♦ Sprinting

8 x 4/1 (10 laps total—refer to page 198 if you need a refresher)

Week Two, Day Five

+ Daily Warmup

  5 Minutes of Naked Turkish Getups

  A few rounds of—
    ▪ Windmill Stick
    ▪ Hip-Flexor Stretch
    ▪ Elevated Roll

+ Strength Training Workout

  One-Arm Press
    ▪ 1-2-3-1-2-3

  15 TRX T Pulls

+ Conditioning Workout

  10 Swings, then 5 Goblet Squats

  10 Swings, then 4 Goblet Squats

  10 Swings, then 3 Goblet Squats

  10 Swings, then 2 Goblet Squats

  10 Swings, then 1 Goblet Squat

  Farmer Walk
    ▪ 30 seconds; 30 seconds; 30 seconds

  Backpack Walk
    ▪ Take a short little excursion with a loaded backpack. Go fifteen minutes to as much as an hour, but don't push it.

Week Two, Days Six and Seven

Rest for two days. On the rest days, I really want at least a half-hour walk, unloaded…a bit of a stroll. I'll keep repeating this point every week.

WEEK THREE

Week Three, Day One

- ◆ Daily Warmup

  5 Minutes of Naked Turkish Getups

  A few rounds of—
    - Windmill Stick
    - Hip-Flexor Stretch
    - Elevated Roll

- ◆ Strength Training Workout

  One-Arm Press
    - 1-2-3-1-2-3-1-2-3

  30 TRX T Pulls

  Goblet Squat
    - 2-3-5-2-3-5-2-3

  100 Swings
    - 5 sets of 20

  Suitcase Carry
    - 15 seconds L/R; 30 seconds L/R; 45 seconds L/R; 15 seconds L/R; 30 seconds L/R

Easy Walk
- Take a nice, easy walk today. I'd love a really long walk, but do what you can.

Week Three, Day Two

♦ Daily Warmup

5 Minutes of Naked Turkish Getups

A few rounds of—
- Windmill Stick
- Hip-Flexor Stretch
- Elevated Roll

Lateral Walk with a Mini-Band
- 40 seconds L/R; 30 seconds L/R; 30 seconds L/R

Backpack Walk
- Again, strive for over an hour on this. You should consider going longer this week and next week, but if you can't get the time in, that's fine. Now, either this week or next week, try to get two loaded walks in one day—ideally, an hour for both walks. I think two one-hour walks would be great on both of these two weeks, but I get it with life and time and everything. Obviously, this is specific conditioning, so every minute you do this will pay off. This is also a great time to practice walking and drinking water, walking and eating, walking and talking and walking and walking.

Can You Go?

Tip: The worst part of watching most fitness TV shows or internet videos is the quest for exhaustion. Form falls apart, the joints are stressed and we just get a sense of sweat and exhaustion. Honestly, it's better long term to strive for elegance and beauty, and let the body adapt, well, beautifully.

Week Three, Day Three

- Daily Warmup

    5 Minutes of Naked Turkish Getups

    A few rounds of—
    - Windmill Stick
    - Hip-Flexor Stretch
    - Elevated Roll

- Strength Training Workout

    See-Saw Press Walk
    - 10 seconds; 15 seconds; 15 seconds

    15 TRX T Pulls

    Goblet Squat
    - 1-2-3-1-2-3

    75 Swings
    - 5 sets of 15

    Judy Bear Hug Walk
    - 1-2-1-1

Week Three, Day Four

+ Daily Warmup

   5 Minutes of Naked Turkish Getups

   A few rounds of—
   - Windmill Stick
   - Hip-Flexor Stretch
   - Elevated Roll

+ Sprinting

   8 x 4/1 (10 laps total)

Week Three, Day Five

+ Daily Warmup

   5 Minutes of Naked Turkish Getups

   A few rounds of—
   - Windmill Stick
   - Hip-Flexor Stretch
   - Elevated Roll

+ Strength Training Workout

   One-Arm Press
   - 1-2-3-1-2-3

   15 TRX T Pulls

+ Conditioning Workout

   15 Swings, then 5 Goblet Squats

   15 Swings, then 4 Goblet Squats

15 Swings, then 3 Goblet Squats

15 Swings, then 2 Goblet Squats

15 Swings, then 1 Goblet Squat

Farmer Walk
- 30 seconds; 60 seconds; 30 seconds

Backpack Walk
- Take a short little excursion with a loaded backpack—fifteen minutes to as much as an hour, but don't push it.

Week Three, Days Six and Seven

Rest for two days—it doesn't matter when you rest, just that you rest. It can be Saturday and Sunday, or it can be Thursday and Sunday. On the rest days, though, do at least a half-hour walk, unloaded…a bit of a stroll. This, also, is important.

WEEK FOUR

Week Four, Day One
♦ Daily Warmup

5 Minutes of Naked Turkish Getups

A few rounds of—
- Windmill Stick
- Hip-Flexor Stretch
- Elevated Roll

♦ Strength Training Workout

One-Arm Press
- 1-2-3-1-2-3-1-2-3

30 TRX T Pulls

Goblet Squat
- 2-3-5-2-3-5-2-3

100 Swings
- 5 sets of 20

Suitcase Carry
- 15 seconds L/R; 30 seconds L/R; 45 seconds L/R; 15 seconds L/R; 30 seconds L/R

Bear Crawls
- 15 minutes

Easy Walk
- Walk 30 minutes in the hiking shoes planned for the trip.

Week Four, Day Two

♦ Daily Warmup

5 Minutes of Naked Turkish Getups

A few rounds of—
- Windmill Stick
- Hip-Flexor Stretch
- Elevated Roll

Lateral Walk with a Mini-Band
- 40 seconds L/R; 40 seconds L/R; 30 seconds L/R

Backpack Walk
- Today, do something inefficient. Take a standard load, but carry some kind of weight in both hands. Two or three pounds is enough—these can be small dumbbells or even water bottles, but cans of soup are too thick. As you walk, for at least an hour, pump your arms. Don't overdo it at the start, but look for a nice rhythm as you go along. If you're wearing a heart rate monitor, you'll see how inefficient this is for hiking, but how big the hit is on the HR. Enjoy.

Tip: As you become more and more efficient, you get less and less benefit. Exercise for fat loss, for example, needs to be as inefficient as possible.

Week Four, Day Three

♦ Daily Warmup

5 Minutes of Naked Turkish Getups

A few rounds of—
- Windmill Stick
- Hip-Flexor Stretch
- Elevated Roll

♦ Strength Training Workout

    See-Saw Press Walk
- 15 second; 15 seconds; 15 seconds

    15 TRX T Pulls

    Goblet Squat
- 1-2-3-1-2-3

    75 Swings
- 5 sets of 15

    Judy Bear Hug Walk
- 1-2-2-1

Week Four, Day Four

♦ Daily Warmup

    5 Minutes of Naked Turkish Getups

    A few rounds of—
- Windmill Stick
- Hip-Flexor Stretch
- Elevated Roll

♦ Sprinting
- 8 x 4/1 (10 laps total)
- *Ideally, this is beginning to look good.*

Week Four, Day Five

- ♦ Daily Warmup

  5 Minutes of Naked Turkish Getups

  A few rounds of—
    - Windmill Stick
    - Hip-Flexor Stretch
    - Elevated Roll

- ♦ Strength Training Workout

  One-Arm Press
    - 1-2-3-1-2-3

  15 TRX T Pulls

- ♦ Conditioning Workout

  15 Swings, then 5 Goblet Squats

  15 Swings, then 4 Goblet Squats

  15 Swings, then 3 Goblet Squats

  15 Swings, then 2 Goblet Squats

  15 Swings, then 1 Goblet Squat

  Farmer Walk
    - 30 seconds; 60 seconds; 30 seconds

  Backpack Walk
    - Just take a short little excursion with a loaded backpack—fifteen minutes to as much as an hour, but don't push it.

Week Four, Days Six and Seven

Rest for two days. Take at least a half-hour walk, unloaded, both days.

WEEK FIVE—PACKING, ASSESSING AND DELOADING WEEK

Points of emphasis this week—

1. Foot care: This is the week you *cannot* have blisters and other minor injuries. Do whatever things you need to do on a daily basis to address foot issues.

2. Begin using sugar-free Metamucil every evening. Under the stress of the challenge, digestion and elimination issues become increasingly impactful. Chuckle away at this advice, but you won't be laughing if you ignore it.

3. Don't get cute on the menu. Don't experiment with new foods or eat at the vendor with a discounted price on day-old sushi.

4. Drink a lot of water and spend some time moving around after you land if the trip involves an air flight. Be sure to have two alarms to wake yourself up, and bring eyeshades and ear plugs if you get lucky enough to room on the same floor as the drunk tourists.

5. It's time to let the arrow fly. Don't add anything. Don't get a deep-tissue massage or spend twelve hours in a sauna if you don't usually do that. You cannot get better in forty-eight hours. Stick with your plan. That plan, the one you've been doing for a few months, is pretty good. Even if it isn't.

6. Have this posted on the front of your brain: *Trust the process*. Trust your training, trust your approach, trust all the work you've done. When something challenges you—and something will—trust the process. You have to let go of the bowstring to let the arrow fly.

Week Five, Day One

- ◆ Daily Warmup

    5 Minutes of Naked Turkish Getups

    A few rounds of—
    - ■ Windmill Stick
    - ■ Hip-Flexor Stretch
    - ■ Elevated Roll

- ◆ Strength Training Workout

    One-Arm Press
    - ■ 2-3-5-2-3-5-2-3

    25 TRX T Pulls

    Goblet Squat
    - ■ 2-3-5-2-3-5-2-3

    100 Swings
    - ■ 5 sets of 20

    Suitcase Carry
    - ■ 15 seconds L/R; 30 seconds L/R; 45 seconds L/R; 60 seconds L/R

    Bear Crawls
    - ■ 15 minutes

Easy Walk
- 60 minutes

Week Five, Day Two

♦ Daily Warmup

5 Minutes of Naked Turkish Getups

A few rounds of—
- Windmill Stick
- Hip-Flexor Stretch
- Elevated Roll

Backpack Walk
- Skip the mini-band walk today, and just do a long backpack walk. Pop out the door and go. Try to sit down and eat a meal on the hike, then pop up and go afterward to get a sense of things. This is the day to test anything new: sunglasses, goofy hat, sunscreen (overrated…just cover up!), shoes, socks or whatever.

Week Five, Day Three

♦ Daily Warmup

5 Minutes of Naked Turkish Getups

A few rounds of—
- Windmill Stick
- Hip-Flexor Stretch
- Elevated Roll

- ◆ Strength Training Workout

  See-Saw Press Walk
  - 15 seconds; 15 seconds; 15 seconds

  15 TRX T Pulls

  Goblet Squat
  - 1-2-3-1-2-3

  75 Swings
  - 5 sets of 15

  Judy Bear Hug Walk
  - 1-2-2-2-1

Week Five, Day Four

- ◆ Daily Warmup

  5 Minutes of Naked Turkish Getups

  A few rounds of—
  - Windmill Stick
  - Hip-Flexor Stretch
  - Elevated Roll

- ◆ Sprinting
  - 4 x 4/1 (5 laps total)

Week Five, Day Five

- ◆ Daily Warmup

  5 Minutes of Naked Turkish Getups

  A few rounds of—
  - Windmill Stick

- Hip-Flexor Stretch
- Elevated Roll

♦ Strength Training Workout

One-Arm Press
- 1-2-3-1-2-3

15 TRX T Pulls

♦ Conditioning Workout

10 Swings, then 5 Goblet Squats

10 Swings, then 4 Goblet Squats

10 Swings, then 3 Goblet Squats

10 Swings, then 2 Goblet Squats

10 Swings, then 1 Goblet Squat

Farmer Walk
- 30 seconds; 60 seconds; 60 seconds

Backpack Walk
- Take a short little excursion with a loaded backpack. Go fifteen minutes to as much as an hour, but don't push it.

Week Five, Days Six and Seven

Rest for two days. Now, I don't care when you rest. It can be Saturday and Sunday, or it can be Thursday and Sunday, or whatever. On the rest days, though, I really want at least a half-hour walk, unloaded. These are important rest days, so relax, but pay attention.

WEEK SIX (PEAK WEEK)

The hay is in the barn and all those other clichés about it being go-time are now appropriate. Listen, you can't do much here except screw up.

The daily warmup is important; you can do it anywhere. If you can't follow this week's program perfectly, that's fine—but get the warmup in every day. The rolling and simple drills of the warmup are specific to traveling, travelers and climbing.

The daily warmup is designed to provide a bit of leeway, some extra room, in terms of the issues travelers have to cope with the most. When you get off the plane and get somewhere you can move around, do these simple movements to gauge how much you got tied up in travel. Touching your toes for a few seconds is going to do little, and may even harm you, versus these rolling and stretching movements.

Week Six, Day One

+ Daily Warmup

    5 Minutes of Naked Turkish Getups

    A few rounds of—
    - Windmill Stick
    - Hip-Flexor Stretch
    - Elevated Roll

+ Strength Training Workout

    One-Arm Press
    - 3-5-2-3

25 TRX T Pulls

Goblet Squat
- 2-3-5-2-3-5

75 Swings
- 5 sets of 15

Suitcase Carry
- 15 seconds L/R; 30 seconds L/R

Easy Walk
- Up to 60 minutes

Week Six, Day Two

♦ Daily Warmup

5 Minutes of Naked Turkish Getups

A few rounds of—
- Windmill Stick
- Hip-Flexor Stretch
- Elevated Roll

Easy Walk
- Go for a walk, if you can, with nothing on your back. Wear the shoes and hiking gear you're planning to use, but just enjoy the stroll. Longer is better today. Keep a notebook and pen with you to take note of the things that come up as you walk.

Week Six, Day Three

- ♦ Daily Warmup

    5 Minutes of Naked Turkish Getups

    A few rounds of—
    - Windmill Stick
    - Hip-Flexor Stretch
    - Elevated Roll

- ♦ Strength Training Workout

    See-Saw Press Walk
    - 15 seconds only

    15 TRX T Pulls

    Goblet Squat
    - 1-2-3

    75 Swings
    - 5 sets of 15

    Easy Walk
    - One or two hours of easy walking, if you can.

Week Six, Day Four

- ♦ Daily Warmup

    5 Minutes of Naked Turkish Getups

    A few rounds of—
    - Windmill Stick
    - Hip-Flexor Stretch

- Elevated Roll

Easy Walk

- Just take an easy walk. If you can add a few easy strides—an easy sprint—that's fine, but don't push it.

Week Six, Day Five

- Daily Warmup

  5 Minutes of Naked Turkish Getups

  A few rounds of—
    - Windmill Stick
    - Hip-Flexor Stretch
    - Elevated Roll

- Strength Training Workout

  One-Arm Press
    - 1-2-3

  10 TRX T Pulls

- Conditioning Workout

  10 Swings, then 5 Goblet Squats

  10 Swings, then 4 Goblet Squats

  10 Swings, then 3 Goblet Squats

  10 Swings, then 2 Goblet Squats

  10 Swings, then 1 Goblet Squat

Backpack Walk

- If you have your actual gear, walk around with your load for fifteen minutes. Search for hot spots on your skin or misloads or potential issues, and fix them now. Something will come up later, no doubt, but let's fix what you can now.

Week Six, Days Six and Seven

Rest for two days. Be sure to take two days completely off before you start hiking. This is called the "two-day lag rule." Soreness is worse two days after a hard session. The day before is no big deal.

Now, climb that mountain!

I included this program to show how simple it is to apply these principles to anything you want to accomplish, from mountain climbing to fat loss. Just remember: Focus on the movements, do them every day and trust in the repetitions.

Appendix 7

Training the College Thrower

WORKING WITH COLLEGE ATHLETES can be fun...and frustrating. Generally, they understand sacrifice and hard work. Sadly, they are also very bright and read everything they can. In other words, these are the kings and queens of BBDs (Bigger, Better Deals).

They tend to enjoy lots of volume and a lot of movements. What they need is intensity, mastery and making the standards of strength. What they want and what they need are often at odds with each other. As you know by now, if I could sum up my evaluation of the issue with most people's training, it would be that what they want and what they need do not line up.

I focus on what my clients *need* to do. I trust they'll slip in all the "other stuff" on their own time. I don't worry about my male throwers working their arms or my female throwers doing ab work. They will.

223

The program I offer is simple. Three days a week, we focus on a full-body lift, a squat and a press. We finish most of the training sessions with a loaded carry. The secret is in the weekly scheme.

I used to make the full-body lift much more complex. I had a long progression of movements that moved from power snatches to power cleans to clean-grip snatches. Each move had three different starting positions and included other variations, too. It was lovely on paper, but it didn't work.

It's a lesson that repeats itself, if I may repeat myself: Some things look good on a chalkboard and are miserable in application. The opposite is true, too, and that's why experience is such a gift to the coach. Sadly, it can be hell on the athlete.

So now we basically snatch or clean. Whatever works with the athletes' body types, time of year, or "how they feel today" is fine with me. Taller kids do more from the knees, and shorter kids seem to want to do more from the floor.

Stress this: Attack your weaknesses, but compete with your strengths. Find those weaknesses, and address them any way you can.

For squats, the list is narrow: back, front or overhead. For pressing, you'll find flat bench, incline, decline and military on the list. Everything is simple and basic.

Our volume day is Day One, which we always do on Mondays. Five sets of five of all three lifts. There are many ways to do five sets of five, but the key is just to do them.

Day Three is eight sets of doubles, and it's best if the athlete adds weight to each set.

Day Five needs a little explanation: It's just one single with 80 percent of the athlete's best lift. Warm up as needed to get there, and then do a single with this medium load. Then, everyone's done. Go home. That's it.

Every month or so, we change the lifts. Follow the dictum, "same, but different." If you had everyone benching, shift to inclines. Over months and years, the load will steadily increase.

Days Two, Four and Six are pure throwing practice, drills or competition, and Day Seven is a refresher.

Day One

+ Throwing practice

+ 5 sets x 5 reps of—
  ◊ Total-Body Lift
  ◊ Squat
  ◊ Press

Day Two

+ Longest duration throwing practice of the week

+ Throwing drills

Day Three

+ 8 sets x 2 reps—
  ◊ Total-Body Lift
  ◊ Squat
  ◊ Press

Day Four

+ Extended warmup

+ Throwing drills

Day Five

+ Warmup

- Easy throwing
- Singles with 80 percent—
  - ◊ Total-Body Lift
  - ◊ Squat
  - ◊ Press

Day Six

- Compete or throw far in training

Day Seven

- Long walk or jog

- Refresh

If there is a secret here, it's this: Try to do this for four or five years. Push yourself away from the idea of easy solutions for elite athletics. After four or five years, we should expect the male athlete to be able to do the following minimums—

- 400-pound bench press
- 250-pound snatch
- 300-pound clean
- 450-pound back squat

These numbers are obtainable for most people with the gifts needed to be a collegiate thrower. If the numbers lag, the off-season might need to be focused on raising any of the specific lifts. As with most elite training programs, the easy thing is getting strong enough—the hard thing is the technical and performance side.

Don't forget that. It's the career.

Appendix 8

It's More Than Just One Day—It's the Career

In Tommy Kono's remarkable second book, *Championship Weightlifting: Beyond Muscle Power,* it's hard to find a page that doesn't contain a great training gem for the interested athlete. Tommy's career is unparalleled. As an Olympic lifter, his gold medals at the Olympics and world championships, his world records and extraordinary career as a coach and author all place him at the top of the game. Many forget, however, that he was also Mr. Universe, a champion bodybuilder.

In the last chapter of his book, Kono writes about being at the right place at the right time. Tommy reviews his life story from his childhood sicknesses to discovering weightlifting at a World War II internment camp—for the record, after you read both of his books, it becomes easier to stop feeling sorry for yourself. Dealing with various ailments, Tommy struggled to learn how to even lift those weights out of the box.

227

Tommy makes an interesting comment, one that almost seems offhand, near the end of the book: "I would train for a weightlifting contest, but as soon as the contest was over, I would immediately start pumping up."

He goes on to discuss that after a few weeks of bodybuilding movements, he'd feel himself becoming interested in heavy movements again. This is a simple idea, and many probably pass over it.

Tommy also recommends lifting in as many Olympic lifting meets as one can during a year. The athlete who follows his recommendations would probably have several intensive six-week periods preparing for an Olympic lifting meet, followed by maybe three to four weeks of pumping.

Don't worry about the specifics; worry about the career.

There is a genius insight here. First, how long can an athlete just do one sport alone?

With basketball, it seems that a small percentage can play year-round for decades and achieve the highest level. They are rewarded with multimillion-dollar contracts. Some nations have massive state-funded sports programs that take literally tens of thousands of young athletes and end up with a handful of champions—or I guess we might call them survivors.

For most of us, though, we should follow Tommy Kono's approach: Train hard, focus on a competition and then move into something complementary. Many throwers, for example, find that entering Highland Games competitions is the perfect tonic to a long track season. Same, but different.

Tommy's great insight seems to hold true decades after his lifting career ended—it's still valuable today.

While hyperspecificity works with the right genetics, the right support system and the right rewards, at the end of the day for most of us there's a need to have a "same, but different" approach.

Unlike peaking programs, alternating naturally between specific and general work seems to lead to a longer, healthier approach to elite sports.

This discussion of training longevity gets us back to the issue of problems versus mysteries. I can show you the basics that worked and will continue to work—the answer to the problem. It's what you learned the first days of school, the first years in your home, and the basics and fundamentals of life, lifting and everything.

But, we all crave mystery. What's the secret pill, sauce, potion or lotion?

Maybe it really is *this*—but generally we already know the answers to the questions. Want to get stronger? Lift weights. Want to lose fat? Cut back on calories. Want to make a difference? Get out in the world and lend a hand.

I'm known for being good at the basics and keeping things simple, and let me tell you—simple ain't easy.

I always joke that the coach who trains himself has an idiot for a client. I was self-coached for years. That's right—I fully admit I'm an idiot.

The problem with self-coaching is that it's too hard to study the person in the mirror and see the whole picture. Sure, you can look over your shoulder, but the reflection will be twisted.

Friends can help. John Price used to remind me daily that "you are only as strong as your weakest link," and we would seek that out. Every preseason, I would chart out my weak points and note them.

Then I'd ignore them.

Finally, I made a decision: I hired Buddy Walker to train me two days a week. He forced me to do things I would have preferred to skip, like conditioning and mobility work. Hiring Buddy as my trainer gave me a great insight: I really don't have enough energy or will to work on my weak points instead of what I like to do and what I'm good at.

I'm not alone. I think we all suffer from this lack of willpower when it comes to our own training.

Don't worry about the specifics; worry about the career.

For More From Dan John—
Wandering Weights: Our Epic Journey Through All Things Heavy

SOMETIMES YOU MISS THE most interesting training-related articles. Sometimes the ideas in the most talked-about articles are confusing. You're not sure what to think.

Sometimes Dan just makes you laugh.

We've gotcha covered! Each Wednesday Dan gives us a short overview of what he's reading and what he's thinking about while he reads. All you have to do to get his weekly review is to sign up.

And when you click the confirmation link, we'll send you a copy of Dan's five-page report on *The Quadrants of Diet and Exercise,* one of his most-discussed training concepts. Enter your email address at the link below to keep up with Dan's conversations.

http://danjohn.net/wandering-weights/

And You Can Also Tap into the Brains of Some of the World's Leading Performance Experts

You can also get free access to information from some of the world's leading performance experts through On Target Publications. You'll get the latest articles, interviews, specials and product release details sent straight to your email.

You'll also get FREE lifetime access to the OTP Vault, which contains articles and videos from experts like Dan John, Gray Cook, Stuart McGill, Sue Falsone, Lorimer Moseley and more.

To get access to the OTP Vault, enter your name and email at the following link.

http://otpbooks.com/Dan-John-Book-Bonus

Acknowledgements

FIRST, WE SHOULD NEVER IGNORE the contributions of Tiffini and my mother and father. I would also be remiss to ignore Dick Notmeyer and Ralph Maughan.

Second, I would like to thank those who allowed me to reinvent myself as a coach after leaving the collegiate and scholastic levels. My hat tips to the Coyote Point Kettlebell Club and those crazies who show up at my door every day here in Murray. A special nod to Dan Martin for being the best kind of mentor—one who leads from the front. In addition, Mike Warren Brown has been a constant companion on my merry trip through the world of strength training.

If I may, I would like to thank the countless people who have emailed, called or visited asking for more clarity. These questions lead to better answers.

Finally, I would like to thank Laree Draper. She volunteered to sell my DVDs more than a decade ago, and then we came up with an idea that maybe I should write a book. My life...and the lives of my children and my grandchildren...were changed by that discussion. I am, and always shall remain, in her debt.

Index

TRX, need for, 98–9
Tsatsouline, Pavel, 69, 100, 132, 141
Turley, Brett, 156
Turner, Dave, 108
Two Test Tubes, The, 149–50

untrained clients, 114

vegetables
    adding to diet, 84
    colorful, 30, 69
vertical growth, 147
"virtual stone soup," 91–2

waist measurement, 49
Walker, Buddy, 229–30
Walsh, Bill, 73
wants, clients', vs. needs, 1–4, 157, 223
warmups, 131–2
water intake, 49, 59–60, 68, 84
weight, assessment of, 25, 48–9
weight lifting, strength training and, 56–7
weight load, correct, 101–4
well-trained clients, 116
White, T.B., 136
Wilde, Oscar, 144
Winters, Bud, 15
Wolf, Robb, 29–30

Secrets About the Author

~Tiffini Hemingway John

IN AUGUST 1987, DAN JOHN was a high school history teacher who drove a rusted Volkswagen Super Beetle with its rear bumper held on by a weight belt. He had sworn off women and dating. He was convinced he would never get married nor have kids.

All that changed one week before his thirtieth birthday. Dan agreed to accompany one of his assistant coaches to a party, where the coach was being set up on a date with a girl named Tiffini Hemingway. That began a whirlwind relationship resulting in a wedding in May of 1988. His fear of never being a father was alleviated in 1990 and again in 1992 with the birth of his daughters.

Dan's favorite holiday is Thanksgiving. He's such a fan that he insists on "practicing" Thanksgiving at least four times a year.

He received an Irish tin whistle as a gift, and practices it every day.

Finally, the man is a crier. He tears up when he's happy, and he tears up when he's sad. Whether he's watching the opening scene of *Love Actually,* or attempting to get through singing a verse of *Danny Boy* to his grandson Danny, you had better make sure there are tissues nearby.

Two of Dan's favorite sayings are, "It's not where you start, it's where you finish" (the John family motto) and "Make a difference."

Dan John is proof positive of both.